Identity

AND THE

Life Cycle

ERIK H. ERIKSON

Identity

AND THE

Life Cycle

W · W · NORTON & COMPANY

New York · London

Published simultaneously in Canada by George J. McLeod Limited, Toronto. Printed in
the United States of America.

Library of Congress Cataloging in Publication Data
Erikson, Erik Homburger, 1902–
  Identity and the life cycle.
  Bibliography: p.
  1. Psychoanalysis.   2. Identity (Psychology)
3. Ego (Psychology)   4. Developmental psychology.
I. Title.
BF175.E7   1979   155   79–9750
ISBN 0–393–01246–8
ISBN 0 393 00949 1—paper edition

2 3 4 5 6 7 8 9 0

Contents

Prefaces

The collection of essays here reissued first appeared in 1959, as monograph 1, volume I, in the series *Psychological Issues,* published by International Universities Press. The references to a "psychological issue" at the beginning and at the end of the original preface, which follows, allude to that publication.

Preface 1 (1959)

The republication of selected papers usually calls for a statement of sufficient reason. This monograph contains writings which are in demand as source material—a demand so persistent and coming from such different professional quarters as to point to a live "psychological issue."

The title states the over-all theme: It is the unity of the human life cycle, and the specific dynamics of each of its stages, as prescribed by the laws of individual development and of social organization. In psychoanalysis this theme has so far not been carried beyond childhood, and a few papers cannot aim to do more than to delineate the specific psychosocial task of youth, namely, the formation of ego identity, and to outline work as yet to be done.

The nature of my papers explains their varying commitment to

theory. The first paper (a selection of clinical notes which ante-
dated and, in fact, provided source material for my book *Childhood
and Society)* illustrates that combination of therapeutic observations and impressions from "applied" work which leads a clinician
to a rethinking of his premises. Application here does not mean
only the use of psychoanalytic hypotheses in other fields—such as
Indian education, war work, and longitudinal child study—but a
sharing of the conditions of observation in these fields. The
clinician approaches such episodical opportunities for communication and service with whatever theory has become implicit in his
observational habits; only gradually does it become apparent that
the extraclinical application suggests a new look at the clinical
theory itself.

The paper "Growth and Crises of the Healthy Personality"
owes its existence to another challenge. A group of experts in child
development, appointed by the U.S. Children's Bureau to prepare for the White House Conference in 1950 an outline of the
verified facts and the promising theories pertaining to mental
health in childhood, asked the writer as a clinician and citizen
how, at that date and for that purpose, he could restate what in his
book *Childhood and Society* had been implied regarding the development of a "healthy personality." The writer overruled his
own misgivings regarding the theoretical prematurity and the
possible misuses of a schema of normality, and, asking Joan
Erikson (as a mother and educator) for assistance, elaborated on
some clinical insights. Insight, of course, is an integral part of a
clinician's work; when spelled out, however, it must include
(rather than pass by) whatever verifiable knowledge, consistent
theory, and therapeutic method are at the clinician's disposal (see
Erikson, 1958b). The paper appears here substantially in the form
in which it was presented to the study group preparing the White
House Conference. However, I have put into italics certain major
points which experience has shown are apt to be ignored, while a
few new footnotes warn against the misuses to which this treatise
has lent itself.

"The Problem of Ego Identity" was addressed to a quite different audience. The program committee of the American Psychoanalytic Association asked me to enlarge on this subject in one section of its yearly midwinter meetings. Here, naturally, references to psychoanalytic theory as well as to therapeutic technique are more numerous, although, here as elsewhere, I have left metapsychological questions to experts in this kind of thinking.

In all their differences, however, the three papers collected here describe three connected steps in clinical thinking: they gradually narrow the issue of psychosocial development from general clinical impressions, to a first outline of psychosocial stages, and finally to a more detailed formulation of one stage, namely, adolescence. Future inquiry must focus on the comparison of several life stages studied in this manner, and must eventually turn to the implications of such studies for the understanding of the whole human life cycle.

Workers from other fields will find in my bibliography references to the transcripts of a number of interdisciplinary meetings in which my concepts were presented and discussed (Erikson, 1951a, 1953, 1955a, 1955b, 1956, 1958c; Erikson and Erikson, 1957). Nowadays, when direct oral and social communication across disciplines and continents is to a large extent replacing the solitary and detailed study of books, a certain amount of repetitiousness, with proper variations, is unavoidable. My books *Childhood and Society* (1950a) and *Young Man Luther* (1958a) delineate how far I myself have been able to carry an integration of clinical and applied approaches. The clinical psychoanalyst, however, will note that only in more recent years have I begun to take up in earnest the problems of clinical evidence (1954, 1958b) and of therapeutic method, in the light of our expanded historical awareness. In this respect, too, this monograph—retracing a section of one clinical worker's itinerary—presents in truth an as yet open psychological issue.

Preface 2 (1979)

If the republication at the end of the 1950's of selected essays written in the preceding two decades called for a "statement of sufficient reason," what can I say in explanation for the reissue of that same publication in this year, 1979—and this although some of the work reported here has, in the meantime, been incorporated in a book, *Identity: Youth and Crisis* (1968)? True, my publisher must know what he is doing when he considers still valid the "sufficient reason" offered in Preface 1, namely, that there seems to be a "persistent demand" for just this compilation of these early essays. I can only confirm this: the whole tone of what I then called a "clinical worker's itinerary" seems to have retained some special appeal to instructors and students in a variety of fields and countries. Maybe, original observations leading to the recognition of a new contextual affinity of phenomena previously considered isolated from each other can lead to what one friend called an "authenticity" of expression that remains worth reading even if some conceptual details continue to be wide open.

In the first edition, and for the purposes of the newly founded *Psychological Issues*, our late friend David Rapaport provided a lengthy introduction, "A Historical Survey of Psychoanalytic Ego Psychology" (1957–1958). Going back to the very beginnings of Freud's thought, he divided the history of ego psychology into four phases, the first one ending in 1897 and the last one beginning in the 1930's with the major works of Anna Freud (1936) and Heinz Hartmann (1939). Rapaport mapped out these phases in great and admirable detail, and his essay has become a solid and independent part of his life work as now studied by a readership which may overlap that of this volume but does not coincide with it. Rapaport's great emphasis on historical and terminological detail, in fact—so my publisher and I have decided—is not indispensable and may be bewildering to many readers who wish first of all to gain an initial understanding of the relationship between the ego psychology of my time and my evolving theory of *psychosocial development*. We therefore have decided to omit the bulk of Rapaport's essay from this reissue.

I would like, however, to excerpt gratefully some of his concluding suggestions concerning the place of my formulations in the fabric of ego psychology:

Hartmann's theory of adaptation includes a generalized theory of reality-relations, which stresses the special role of social relations (Hartmann, 1939; Hartmann and Kris, 1945; Hartmann, Kris, and Loewenstein, 1951). Yet it does not provide a specific and differentiated psychosocial theory. . . .

Erikson centers on the epigenesis of the ego (Erikson, 1937; 1940a), on the theory of reality-relationships (1945), and especially on the elaboration of the theory of the role of social reality (1950b), and these are the core of his psychosocial theory of development (1950a), which complements Freud's theory of the third phase and Hartmann's elaboration of it.

Erikson's theory outlines *the sequence of phases of ego epigenesis* (1950b) and thus particularizes Hartmann's concept of autonomous ego development, which generalized Freud's conception of the development of anxiety.

This sequence of the phases of ego development parallels that of libido development (1950a, Chapter 2), and goes beyond it and spans *the whole life cycle* (Chapter 7). This conception is the first in the history of psychoanalytic theory to encompass those phases of the life cycle which are customarily subsumed under the single concept of genital maturity, and to provide tools for their investigation. . . .

The crucial characteristic of this psychosocial theory of ego development, and of Hartmann's adaptation theory (in contrast to the "culturalist" theories) is that they offer a conceptual explanation of the individual's social development by tracing the unfolding *of the genetically social character of the human individual* in the course of his encounters with the social environment at each phase of his epigenesis. Thus it is not assumed that societal norms are grafted upon the genetically asocial individual by "disciplines" and "socialization," but that the society into which the individual is born makes him its member by influencing *the manner in which* he solves the tasks posed by each phase of his epigenetic development. . . .

Erikson's theory (like much of Freud's) ranges over phenomenological, specifically clinical psychoanalytic and general psychoanalytic-psychological propositions, without systematically differentiating between them. Correspondingly, the conceptual status of this theory's terms is so far unclear. To systematize this theory and to clarify the conceptual status of its terms is a task for ego psychology in the future.

Erikson's contributions constitute an organic extension of Freud's theory and they and Hartmann's contributions are consistent with and complementary to each other. Yet Erikson related his theory in an explicit fashion mainly to the concepts of Freud's id psychology, less to the concepts of Freud's ego psychology, and only slightly to Hartmann's theory. Nor did Hartmann attempt to formulate the relation between his and Erikson's theory. Here a task of integration faces ego psychology.

These passages obviously provided for the reader of the monograph a sympathetic review of the theoretical unification I was preparing in the three essays. What even Rapaport in conclusion must characterize as the unclear theoretical status of my theory's terms applies most significantly to the term central to this publication but used less in my subsequent work, namely, "ego identity." For my itinerary through issues of identity and of the life cycle does not come to rest in reaching a foothold in existing ego psychology. Rather, as Rapaport indicates in passing, this itinerary is, in these very pages, leading to a psychoanalytic theory of psychosocial development, the presently existing elements of which I have assembled only recently at the request of the National Institute of Mental Health (in press). This psychosocial orientation, furthermore, has become part of a historical one which would force us eventually to view the ego's functioning (as well as our attempts to grasp the nature of what we have been calling "ego") as processes underlying a historical relativity. This trend was already obvious in my books *Childhood and Society* (1950a, revised 1963) and *Young Man Luther* (1958a), which had been published at the time of the monograph's appearance.

As its opening paragraph indicates, this publication is a first and searching attempt to approach the changing ethos of historical periods from the point of view of clinical observation. But this can only mean to underscore (sometimes rather one-sidedly) the symptomatology of some of the psychological disorders which during a given period prevail in a substantial minority of the population and thus represent the *epidemiological counterpart* to the *dominant ethos* of a period's patterns of communality and productivity. The question of how to account eventually for the balance of the inspiring and the confusing forces characteristic for a given period of history I have been able to approach only in some further

biographic work which describes the interaction of leaders of
guiding genius with their times: Gandhi taking charge of India's
destiny in his middle years (1969) and Jefferson's assumption of a
pervasive role in the emergence of the American identity (1974).
The interrelation of styles of individuality and communality in
the patterns of daily life, in turn, is approached in a book on play,
ritualization, and politics (1977).

All this work can be said to be tending toward formulations of
the complementary interplay of life history and history. Correspondingly, acute clinical observations and formulations can always be seen to be guided concomitantly by a number of discern-
ible historical processes. In the concentration on any one life
theme such as identity we may well be guided by motives rooted
in our own *personal history*. This I had the occasion to outline in the
autobiographic part of an essay (1975) in which I joined men and
women of different scientific and humanistic fields in reflections
on the origins of one of our most decisive concepts in our personal
and professional lives. At the same time, however, the *therapeutic*
and *theoretical* course of my field as outlined above by Rapaport
and substantiated below in my clinical episodes strongly pointed
to the need for an identity concept—as did, with an unforgettable
crescendo, the *historical aggravation* of identity problems in the
youth of the sixties, when I, in fact, was primarily a college
teacher (1963).

The publication here reissued, however, concentrates on a
theme fundamental to all these perspectives, namely, the place of
psychosocial identity within the developmental logic of the
human life cycle—as conceived in the 1940's and 1950's.

Identity
AND THE
Life Cycle

1

Ego Development
and Historical Change

Clinical Notes

MEN WHO SHARE an ethnic area, a historical era, or an economic
pursuit are guided by common images of good and evil. Infinitely
varied, these images reflect the elusive nature of historical change;
yet in the form of contemporary social models, of compelling
prototypes of good and evil, they assume decisive concreteness in
every individual's ego development. Psychoanalytic ego psychology has not matched this concreteness with sufficient theoretical
specificity. On the other hand, students of history continue to
ignore the simple facts that all individuals are borne by mothers;
that everybody was once a child; that people and peoples begin in
their nurseries; and that society consists of individuals in the
process of developing from children into parents.

Only psychoanalysis and social science together can eventually
chart the life cycle interwoven throughout with the history of the
community. To this end, the present collection of clinical notes

The original version of this paper appeared in *The Psychoanalytic Study of the Child*, 2:359–
396, 1946.

offers questions, illustrations, and theoretical considerations concerning the relation of the child's ego to the historical prototypes of the day.

GROUP IDENTITY AND EGO IDENTITY

1

Freud's original formulations concerning the ego and its relation to society necessarily depended on the general trend of his analytic argument at the time on the sociological formulations of his era. The fact that Freud, for his first group-psychological discussions, quoted the postrevolutionary French sociologist Le Bon has left its mark on consequent psychoanalytic discussions of "multitudes" of men. As Freud recognized, Le Bon's "masses" were society of the rebound, shiftless mobs enjoying the anarchy between two stages of society and, at their best and worst, leader-led mobs. Such mobs exist; their definition stands. However, there is a wide gap between these sociological observations and the material secured by the psychoanalytic method—namely, individual history reconstructed from the evidence of transferences and countertransferences, in a therapeutic situation *à deux*. The resulting methodological gap has perpetuated in psychoanalytic thought an artificial differentiation between the individual-within-his-family (or seemingly surrounded by projections of his family constellation on the "outer world") and the "individual-in-the-mass," submerged in an "indistinct aggregate" of men.[1] The phenomenon and the concept of *social organization*, and its bearing on the individual ego was, thus, for the longest time, shunted off by patronizing tributes to the existence of "social factors."

In general, the concept of the ego was first delineated by previous definitions of its better-known opposites, the biological id and the sociological "masses": the ego, the individual center of organized experience and reasonable planning, stood endangered by both the anarchy of the primeval instincts and the lawlessness of the group spirit. One might say that where Kant gave as the coordinates of the moral burgher, "the stars above him" and "the moral law within him," the early Freud placed his fearful ego between the id within him and the mob around him.

To take account of encircled man's precarious morality, Freud instituted within the ego the ego ideal or superego. The emphasis, at first, was again on the foreign burden which was thus imposed on the ego. The superego, so Freud pointed out, is the internalization of all the restrictions to which the ego must bow. It is forced upon the child *("von aussen aufgenötigt")* by the critical influence of the parents, and later, by that of professional educators, and of what to the early Freud was a vague multitude of fellow men *("die unbestimmte Menge der Genossen")* making up the "milieu" and "public opinion" (Freud, 1914).

Surrounded by such mighty disapproval, the child's original state of naïve self-love is said to be compromised. He looks for models by which to measure himself, and seeks happiness in trying to resemble them. Where he succeeds he achieves *self-esteem*, a not too convincing facsimile of his original narcissism and sense of omnipotence.

These early conceptual models have never ceased to determine the trend of discussions and aims of practice in clinical psychoanalysis.[2] The focus of psychoanalytic research, however, has shifted to a variety of genetic problems. From the study of the ego's dissipation in an amorphous multitude or in a leader-mob, we have turned to the problem of the infantile ego's origin in organized social life. Instead of emphasizing what social organization denies the child, we wish to clarify what it may first grant to the infant, as it keeps him alive and as, in administering to his needs in a specific way, it seduces him to its particular life style. Instead of accepting the oedipus trinity as an irreducible schema for man's irrational conduct, we are striving for greater specificity by exploring the way in which social organization codetermines the structure of the family; for, as Freud said toward the end of his life, ". . . what is operating [in the superego] is not only the personal qualities of these parents but also everything that produced a determining effect upon themselves, the tastes and standards of the social class in which they live and the characteristics and traditions of the race from which they spring" (1938, pp. 122–123).

2

Freud showed that sexuality begins with birth; he has also given us the tools for the demonstration of the fact that social life begins with each individual's beginnings.

Some of us have applied these tools to the study of so-called primitive societies where child training is integrated with a well-defined economic system and a small and static inventory of social prototypes.[3] Child training in such groups, so we concluded, is the method by which a group's basic ways of organizing experience (its group identity, as we called it) is transmitted to the infant's early bodily experiences and, through them, to the beginnings of his ego.

Let me first illustrate the concept of group identity by a brief reference to anthropological observations made by Mekeel and myself some years ago. We described how in one segment of the re-education of the American Indian, the Sioux Indians' historical identity of the—now defunct—Buffalo hunter stands counterposed to the occupational and class identity of his re-educator, the American civil service employee. We pointed out that the identities of these groups rest on extreme differences in geographic and historical perspectives (collective ego-space-time) and on radical differences in economic goals and means (collective life plan).

In the remnants of the Sioux Indians' identity, the prehistoric past is a powerful psychological reality. The conquered tribe behaved as if guided by a life plan consisting of passive resistance to the present which does fail to reintegrate the identity remnants of the economic past; and of dreams of restoration, in which the future would lead back into the past, time would again become ahistoric, space unlimited, activity boundlessly centrifugal, and the buffalo supply inexhaustible. Their federal educators, on the other hand, preached a life plan with centripetal and localized goals: homestead, fireplace, bank account—all of which receive their meaning from a life plan in which the past is overcome, and in which the full measure of fulfillment in the present is sacrificed to an ever higher standard of living in the (ever removed) future. The road to this future is not outer restoration but inner reform.

Obviously every item of human experience as lived by a member of one of these groups, and as shared or debated by memebers of both groups, must be defined according to its place on the coordinates of these interpenetrating plans.

Primitive tribes have a direct relation to the sources and means of production. Their tools are extensions of the human body. Children in these groups participate in technical and in magic pursuits; to them, body and environment, childhood and culture may be full of dangers, but they are all one world. The inventory of social prototypes is small and static. In our world, machines, far from remaining an extension of the body, destine whole human organizations to be extensions of machinery; magic serves intermediate links only; and childhood becomes a separate segment of life with its own folklore. The expansiveness of civilization, together with its stratification and specialization, force children to base their ego models on shifting, sectional, and contradictory prototypes.

3

The growing child must derive a vitalizing sense of reality from the awareness that his individual way of mastering experience (his ego synthesis) is a successful variant of a group identity and is in accord with its space-time and life plan.

A child who has just found himself able to walk seems not only driven to repeat and to perfect the act of walking by libidinal pleasure in the sense of Freud's locomotor erotism; or by the need for mastery in the sense of Ives Hendrick's work principle; he also becomes aware of the new status and stature of "he who can walk," with whatever connotation this happens to have in the coordinates of his culture's life plan—be it "he who will go far," or "he who will be upright," or "he who might go too far." To be "one who can walk" becomes one of the many steps in child development which through the coincidence of physical mastery and cultural meaning, of functional pleasure and social recognition, contribute to a more realistic self-esteem. By no means only a narcissistic corroboration of infantile omnipotence (that can be had more cheaply), this self-esteem grows to be a conviction that the ego is learning effective steps toward a tangible collective future, that it is developing into a defined ego within a social reality. This sense I wish to call *ego identity*. I shall try to clarify it as a subjective experience and as a dynamic fact, as a group-psychological phenomenon and—in the bulk of this paper—as a subject for clinical investigation.

The conscious feeling of having a *personal identity* is based on two simultaneous observations: the immediate perception of one's selfsameness and continuity in time; and the simultaneous perception of the fact that others recognize one's sameness and continuity. What I propose to call ego identity concerns more than the mere fact of existence, as conveyed by personal identity; it is the ego quality of this existence.

Ego identity, then, in its subjective aspect, is the awareness of the fact that there is a selfsameness and continuity to the ego's synthesizing methods and that these methods are effective in safeguarding the sameness and continuity of one's meaning for others.

4

While it was a step of inestimable import when Freud applied contemporaneous concepts of physical energy to psychology, the resultant theory that instinctual energy is transferred, displaced, transformed in analogy to the preservation of energy in physics no longer suffices to help us manage the data which we have learned to observe.

It is here that ego concepts must close a gap. We must find the nexus of social images and of organismic forces—and this not merely in the sense that here images and forces are, as the saying goes, "interrelated." More than this: the mutual complementation of ethos and ego, of group identity and ego identity, puts a greater common potential at the disposal of both ego synthesis and social organization.

When a Sioux Indian—at the height of his religious endeavors—drives little sticks through his breast, ties the sticks to a rope, the rope to a pole, and then (in a peculiar trance) dances backwards until the rope tightens and the sticks split his breast, so that the gushing blood runs freely down his body, we find a meaning in his extreme behavior: he is turning against himself some first provoked, then energetically frustrated infantile impulses, a "fixation" on which we found to be of decisive relevance in the Sioux's group identity and in his individual development.[4] This ritual puts "id" and "superego" in clear opposition, as do the abortive rituals of our neurotic patients. It makes similar sense when a Yurok man, having been with a woman, proceeds to heat himself by the fire of the sweathouse until he is supple enough to squeeze through an oval opening in the wall, only to jump into the cold river; whereupon he considers himself again pure and strong enough to net the sacred salmon. Here, obviously, self-esteem and inner security are restored by atonement. The same Indians, when indulging in promiscuous intercourse after having achieved the yearly communal engineering feat of bridging the river with a dam that yields a whole winter's supply of salmon, apparently experience the manic relief of orgiastic excess, which, once a year, throws atonement to the winds. But if we try to define the state of relative equilibrium between these better-known extremes, if we ask what characterizes an Indian when he does not do much more than just calmly be an Indian, bent on the daily chores of the year's cycle, our description lacks a fitting frame of reference. We look for small signs of the fact that man, anywhere, anytime, betrays in minute emotional and ideational changes an ever-present conflict manifested in a change of mood from a vague anxious depression through what Freud referred to as "a certain in-between stage" to heightened well-being—and back *("von einer übermässigen Gedrücktheit durch einen gewissen Mittelzustand zu einem erhöhten Wohlbefinden")*. But is this in-between stage dynamically so unimportant that it can be defined by pointing out what it is not; by stating that neither a manic nor a depressive trend is, at the time, clearly noticeable, that a momentary lull exists on the battlefield of the ego, that the superego is temporarily nonbelligerent and that the id has agreed to an armistice?

The necessity for defining the relative equilibrium between various "states of mind" became acute in the need to appraise morale in war. I had an opportunity to make a few observations on one of the more extreme milieus of human endeavor, namely, life on submarines (Erikson, 1940b). Here emotional plasticity and social resourcefulness are put to a high test. The heroic expectations and phallic-locomotor fantasies with which an adolescent volunteer approaches life on a submarine are on the whole not verified in the small chores and in the constricted space of his daily experience on board and in the relatively blind, deaf, and dumb role demanded of him in action. The extreme interdependence with the crew and the mutual responsibility for comfort and life under prolonged conditions of extreme hardship soon supersede the original fantasies. Crew and captain establish a symbiosis not governed by official regulations alone. With astonishing tact and native wisdom silent arrangements are made by which the captain becomes sensory system, brains, and conscience for the whole submerged organism of minutely tuned machinery and humanity; and by which the crew members mobilize in themselves compensatory mechanisms (for example, in the collective use of the generously provided food) permitting the crew to stand monotony and yet to be ready for instant action. Such automatic mutual adaptations to extreme milieus make "analytical sense" primarily where a seeming regression to a primal horde, and to a kind of oral lethargy, can be traced. Yet, if we ask why men choose such a life, why they stick to it in spite of incredible monotony and occasional nightmarish danger, and above all why they function in good health and high spirits, we do not have a satisfactory dynamic answer. In psychiatric discussions it is not infrequently suspected—on the evidence of mere analogies—that whole units, crews, and occupational groups are regressive, or motivated by latent homosexual or psychopathic tendencies.

Yet what the submarine man on the job, the Indian at work, and the growing child have in common with all men who feel at one with what they are doing when and where they are doing it is akin to that "in-between state" which we wish our children would preserve as they grow older; and which we want our patients to gain when the "synthetic function of the ego" (Nunberg, 1931) is restored. We know that when this is achieved, play becomes freer, health radiant, sex more adult, and work more meaningful. Having applied psychoanalytic concepts to group problems we feel that a clearer understanding of the mutual complementation of ego synthesis and social organization may help us to appraise therapeutically a psychological middle range, the expansion and cultivation of which on ever higher levels of human organization is the aim of all therapeutic endeavor, social and individual.

EGO PATHOLOGY AND HISTORICAL CHANGE

1

A child has quite a number of opportunities to identity himself, more or less experimentally, with real or fictitious people of either sex, with habits, traits, occupations, and ideas. Certain crises force him to make radical selections. However, the historical era in which he lives offers only a limited number of socially meaningful models for workable combinations of identification fragments. Their usefulness depends on the way in which they simultaneously meet the requirements of the organism's maturational stage and the ego's habits of synthesis.

The desperate intensity of many a child's symptom expresses

the necessity to defend a budding ego identity which to the child promises to integrate the rapid changes taking place in all areas of his life. What to the observer looks like an especially powerful manifestation of naked instinct is often only a desperate plea for the permission to synthesize and sublimate in the only way possible. We therefore can expect the young patient to respond only to therapeutic measures which will help him to complete the prerequisites for the successful formation of his original ego identity. Therapy and guidance may attempt to substitute more desirable identifications for undesirable ones, but the total configuration of the ego identity remains unalterable.[5]

I am thinking here of the son of an ex-German soldier who emigrated to this country because he could not accept Nazism or was unacceptable to it. His little son had hardly time to absorb Nazi indoctrination before he came to this country, where, like most children, he took to Americanization like a duck to water. Gradually, however, he developed a neurotic rebellion against all authority. What he said about the "older generation" and how he said it was clearly taken from Nazi leaves which he had never read; his behavior was an unconscious one-boy-Hitler-youth rebellion. A superficial analysis revealed that the boy in identifying with the slogans of the Hitler youths identified himself with his father's aggressors, according to the oedipal principle.

At this point, the boy's parents decided to send him to a military school. I expected him to rebel violently. Instead, a marked change came over the boy the moment he was handed a uniform with the promise of gold bars, stars, and rank. It was as if these military symbols effected a sudden and decisive change in his inner economy. The boy was now an unconscious Hitler youth wrapped up in an American prototype: the military schoolboy. The father, a mere civilian, now was neither dangerous nor important.

Somewhere, however, it had been this same father and related father surrogates who with unconscious gestures (Erikson, 1942) (especially when speaking of military exploits during the First World War) had helped establish in this boy the military prototype which is a part of many a European's group identity, and in the German mind has the special significance of being one of the few thoroughly German and highly developed identities. As a historical focus of the family's general trend of identifications the military identity continues to exist unconsciously in those who are excluded from its consummation by political developments.[6]

The subtler methods by which children are induced to accept historical or actual people as prototypes of good and evil have hardly been studied. Minute displays of emotion such as affection, pride, anger, guilt, anxiety, sexual tension (rather than the words used, the meanings intended, or the philosophy implied), transmit to the human child the outlines of what really counts in his world, i.e., the variables of his group's space-time and the perspectives of its life plan.

Equally undefined are the minute socioeconomic and cultural *panics* which involve the family, causing individual regressions to infantile atonements and a reactionary return to more primitive moral codes. As such panics coincide in time and in dynamic quality with one of the child's psychosexual crises, they share in the determination of his neurosis: every neurosis is shared panic, isolated anxiety, and somatic tension all at once.

We observe, for instance, that in our guilt-culture, individuals and groups, whenever they perceive that their socioeconomic status is in danger, unconsciously behave as if inner dangers (temptations) had really called forth the threatening disaster. As a consequence, not only individual regressions to early guilt feelings and atonements take place, but also a reactionary return to the content and to the form of historically earlier principles of behavior. The implicit moral code becomes more restricted, more magic, more exclusive, more intolerant, etc. What patients persistently describe as their childhood milieu often is the condensation of a few selected periods in which too many simultaneous changes resulted in a panicky atmosphere.

In the case of another five-year-old boy, who produced convulsions after a number of coincidental experiences all concerning aggression and death, the idea of violence had received its problematic meaning from the following trends in the family history. The father was an Eastern European Jew whom the mild and meek grandparents had taken as a five-year-old to the New York East Side, where he could survive only by superimposing on his childhood identity that of a guy who hits first. This rule he built into our patient's identity, not without indicating how much it had cost him. Having survived with reasonable economic success, however, he then opened a store on the main street of a small Yankee town and moved into a residential neighborhood where he had to revoke his initial instructions and to impress his now cocky and inquisitive little boy, pleadingly and threateningly, with the fact that a shopkeeper's son should treat the Gentiles gently. This change of identities occurred in the midstream of the boy's phallic-locomotor stage, when he needed clear directions and new opportunities of expression—and incidentally at an age analogous to that at which the father had been the victim of migration. The family panic ("let's be gentle or else we will lose ground"), the individual anxiety ("how can I be gentle if all I have learned is to be tough and when I must be tough to feel safe?"), the oedipal problem of managing and diverting aggression against the father, and the somatic tension caused by undirected rage—these were all specific to one another, causing a short circuit instead of the mutual regulation which should dominate simultaneous changes in organism, environment, and ego. His epileptic reaction became manifest.

2

In the analysis of adults the historical prototypes which determined infantile ego-identity crises appear in specific transferences and in specific resistances.

The following excerpt from the case history of an adult illustrates the relationship of such an infantile crisis to the patient's adult life style.

A dancer, of considerable good looks (although extremely small stature), developed the annoying symptom of having to hold her torso so rigidly upright that dancing became awkward and ungainly. The analysis proved her hysterical erectness to be a break-through of a penis envy which had been provoked in childhood along with an otherwise well-sublimated exhibitionism. The patient was the only daughter of a second-generation German-American, a successful businessman given to a certain exhibitionistic individualism, which included a great pride in his powerful physique. He insisted on an erect posture (probably no longer consciously Prussian) on the part of his blond sons, but did not require the same from his dark-skinned daughter; in fact, he did not seem to see much worth exhibiting in the female body. This contributed to other motivations in the patient's dancing the overpowering wish to exhibit an "improved" posture which resembled the caricature of Prussian ancestors whom she had never seen.

The historical anchoring of such symptoms is clarified by the analysis of the resistances with which the symptom is defended.

The patient, who in her conscious thoughts as well as in her positive transference drew a parallel between the father's and the analyst's tall and "Nordic" physiques, to her great dismay found herself dreaming of the analyst as a small, dirty, crumpled-up Jew. With this image of low birth and weak masculinity, she attempted to disqualify him from the right to explore the secret of her symptom, namely, the danger to her fragile ego identity emanating from the association of her sexual conflicts with an unruly pair of historical prototypes, an *ideal* prototype (German, tall, phallic) and an *evil* prototype (Jewish, dwarfish, castrated, female). The patient's ego identity had attempted to subsume this dangerous alternative in the role of the radically modern dancer: a creative gesture which in its defensive aspects constituted an exhibitionistic protest against the social and sexual inferiority of women. Her symptom betrays the fact that the father's exhibitionism, as well as his prejudices, because they were inculcated into the patient through the sensual testimony of the oedipus complex, had retained a dangerous degree of disturbing power in her unconscious.

It is usual in our culture that the unconscious evil identity (that which the ego is most afraid to resemble) is composed of the images of the violated (castrated) body, the ethnic outgroup, and the exploited minority. Although it manifests itself in a great variety of syndromes, this association is all-pervasive, in men and women, in majorities and minorities, and in all classes of a given national or cultural unit. For the ego, in the course of its synthesizing efforts, attempts to subsume the most powerful ideal and evil prototypes (the final contestants, as it were) and with them the whole existing imagery of superior and inferior, good and bad, masculine and feminine, free and slave, potent and impotent, beautiful and ugly, fast and slow, tall and small, in a simple alternative, in order to make one battle and one strategy out of a bewildering number of skirmishes. In this connection, the latent image of the more homogeneous past exerts it reactionary influence in specific resistances; we must study it, so that we may understand the historical basis of the accentuated alternative the patient's ego is searching for.

Unconscious associations of ethnic alternatives with moral and sexual ones are a necessary part of any group formation. Psychoanalysis, in studying them, perfects its therapeutic methods in individual cases and, at the same time, contributes to the knowledge of the unconscious concomitants of prejudice.[7]

3

Therapeutic efforts as well as attempts at social reform verify the sad truth that in any system based on suppression, exclusion, and exploitation, the suppressed, excluded, and exploited unconsciously believe in the evil image which they are made to represent by those who are dominant.[8]

I once saw in consultation a tall, intelligent ranch owner, who was influential in Western agriculture. Nobody but his wife knew that he was born a Jew and raised in a Jewish street in a large city. His life, while outwardly successful, was made uncomfortable by a network of compulsions and phobias which, in analysis, proved to reproduce and to superimpose on his free movements in Western valleys the outline of the neighborhood in which he grew up.

His friends and adversaries, his elders and his inferiors, all un-knowingly played the roles of the German boys or the Irish gangs who had made the little Jewish boy miserable on his daily walk to school, which led him from an isolated and more refined Jewish street through the hostile remnants of tenements and gang warfare to the shortlived haven of the democratic classroom. This man's analysis provided a sad commentary on the fact that Streicher's image of an evil Jewish identity does not surpass that harbored by many a Jew who—with paradoxical results—may still try to live it down in an area where in view of what he is, his past would be relatively unimportant.

The patient in question sincerely felt that the only true savior for the Jews would be a plastic surgeon. In the body ego of such cases of morbid ego identity, those body parts which are supposed to be of strategic importance in the characterization of the race (in the last case, the nose; in that of the dancer, the backbone) play a role similar to that of the afflicted limb in a cripple and that of the genitals in neurotics in general. The body part in question has a different ego tonus; it is felt to be larger and heavier, or smaller and disembodied; in both cases it seems dissociated from the whole of the body, while seeming to loom dominantly in the center of the attention of others. In cases of morbid ego identity and in cripples, there are dreams where the dreamer unsuccess-fully tries to hide the painfully spotlighted body part, and others where he accidentally loses it.

What may be called an individual's ego space-time thus pre-serves the social topology of his childhood surroundings as well as the outline of his body image. To study both it is essential to correlate a patient's childhood history with the history of his family's sedentary residence in prototypal areas (East), in "back-ward" areas (South), or in "forward" areas (Western and Northern frontier), as these areas were gradually incorporated into the American version of the Anglo-Saxon cultural identity; his fami-ly's migration from, through, and to areas which, at various periods, may have represented the extreme sedentary or the ex-treme migratory pole of the developing American character; the family's religious conversions or diversions, with their class implications; abortive attempts at becoming standardized on a class level and the loss or abandonment of that level; and most of all, that individual or family segment which, whatever they were doing and wherever they were doing it, provided the last strong sense of cultural identity.

4

A compulsive patient's grandfather, now deceased, was a business man who built a mansion in a downtown district of an *Eastern metropolis*. His will demands that the mansion should stand and remain the family's castle even though skyscrapers and apartment houses are mushrooming all around it. The mansion becomes a somewhat sinister symbol of conservatism, telling the world that the X's need neither to move nor to sell, neither to expand nor to rise. The conveniences of modern travel are accepted only as comfortably insulated pathways between the mansion and its extensions: the club, the summer home, the private school, Harvard, etc. The grandfather's picture hangs over the fireplace, a little bulb eternally lighting the rosiness of the cheeks in his generally powerful and contented countenance. His "individualistic" ways in business, his almost primeval power over the fate of his children, are known but not questioned; rather they are overcompensated for by a sensitive show of respect, scrupulousness, and thrift. The grandsons know that in order to find an identity of their own they have to break out of the mansion, so to speak, and join the mad striving which has engulfed the neighborhood. Some do, not without taking the mansion with them as an internalized pattern, a basic ego space, which has determined their defense mechanism of proud and pained withdrawal, and their symptoms of obsessiveness and of sexual anesthesia. Their psychoanalyses last inordinately long, partially because the analyst's four walls become the new mansion; the analyst's contemplative silence and his theoretical approach, a new edition of the mansion's ritualistic isolation. Further resistances become plain in dreams and associations. The curative effect of the patient's politely "positive" transference ends where the reticence of the analyst seems to resemble the restrained father rather than the ruthless grandfather. The father image, it appears (and with it the transference), is split up; the image of the weak and mild father of today is isolated from the oedipal father image, which is fused with that of the powerful grandfather. As the analysis approaches this double image, fantasies appear which make plain the grandfather's overwhelming importance for the patient's real ego identity. They betray the violent sense of power, the fury of superiority which makes it hard for these overtly inhibited people to enter economic competition except on terms of prearranged superior privileges. These men, of the once highest strata, join those from the very lowest ones in being the truly disinherited in American life; from where they are there is no admission to free competition, unless they have the strength to start all over. If not, they often resist cure because it implies a change in ego identity, an ego resynthesis on the terms of changed economic history.

The only way of breaking through this deep resignation is serious attention to memories which show (what the child knew) that the grandfather really was a simple man, and that he fulfilled his place not by force of some primeval power, but because history favored his capabilities.

For a *Western* grandfather, I refer to a previously published case (Erikson, 1945, p. 349). Consider a boy whose grandparents came West, "where seldom is heard a discouraging word." The grandfather, a powerful and powerfully driven man, seeks ever new and challenging engineering tasks in widely separated regions. When the initial challenge is met, he hands the task over to others, and moves on. His wife sees him only for an occasional impregnation. According to a typical family pattern, his sons cannot keep pace with him and are left as respectable settlers by the wayside. To express their change of life style in fitting slogans, one would have to state that from an existence characterized by the slogan "let's get the hell out of here," they turn to one expressing the determination "let's stay—and keep the bastards out." The grandfather's only daughter (the patient's mother) alone remains identified with him. This very identification, however, does not permit her to take a husband equal to her strong father. She marries a weak man and settles down. She brings her boy up to be God-fearing and industrious. He becomes reckless and shifting at times, depressed at others: somewhat of a juvenile delinquent now, later maybe a more enjoyable Westerner, with alcoholic moods.

What his worried mother does not know is that she herself all through his childhood has belittled the sedentary father; has decried the lack of mobility, geographic and social, of her marital existence; has idealized the grandfather's exploits; but has also reacted with panicky punitiveness to any display of friskiness in the boy, which was apt to disturb the now well-defined neighborhood.

A woman from the *Middle West*, rather unusually feminine and sensitive, uses a visit with relatives in the West to consult the writer concerning a general feeling of affective constriction and an all-pervasive mild anxiety. During an exploratory analysis she seems almost lifeless. Only after weeks, on rare occasions, is she overcome by a flood of associations, all concerning sudden, horrid impressions of sex or death. Many of these memories emerge not from unconscious depths, but from an isolated corner of her consciousness, where are boarded off all those matters which on occasion had broken through the orderly factualness of the upper-middle-class surroundings of her childhood. This mutual isolation of life segments is similar to that met with in compulsive neurotics anywhere; but in some regions it is more; it is a way of life, an ethos, which in our patient had become truly uncomfortable only because at the moment she was being courted by a European and was trying to envisage life in a cosmopolitan atmosphere. She felt attracted, but at the same time inhibited; her imagination was vividly provoked, but restrained by anxiety. Her bowels reflected this ambivalence by an alternation of constipation and diarrhea. One gained the impression of a general inhibition rather than a basic impoverishment of imagination in matters both sexual and social.

The patient's dreams gradually revealed a hidden source of

unemployed vitality. While she seemed pained and lifeless in her free associations, her dream life became humorous and imaginative in an almost autonomous way. She dreamed of entering quiet church congregations in a flaming red dress, and of throwing stones through respectable windows. But her most colorful dreams put her into Civil War days—on the Confederate side. The climax was a dream in which she sat on a toilet, set off by low partitions in the middle of a tremendous ballroom, and waved to elegantly dressed couples of Confederate officers and Southern ladies who swirled around her to the sounds of powerful brass.

These dreams helped unearth an isolated part of her childhood, namely, the gentle warmth awarded her by her grandfather, a Confederate veteran. His world was a fairy tale of the past. But for all its formalism, the grandfather's patriarchal masculinity and gentle affection had been experienced through the child's hungry senses and had proved more immediately reassuring to her searching ego than either the father's or the mother's promises of standardized success. With the grandfather's death the patient's affects went dead because they were part of an abortive ego-identity formation which failed to receive nourishment either in the form of affection or of social rewards.

The psychoanalytic treatment of women with a prominent ego-identity remnant of the *Southern lady* (an identity which pervades more than one class or race) seems complicated by special resistances. To be sure, our patients are dislodged Southerners, their ladyhood a defense, almost a symptom. Their wish for treatment finds its limits in three ideas, which are all connected with the particular provisions in Southern culture for safeguarding caste and race identity by imposing the prototype of the lady on the small girl.

There is, first, a pseudoparanoid suspicion that life is a series of critical tests when vicious gossips attempt to stack up minor weaknesses and blemishes against the Southern woman—toward a final judgment: to be—or not to be—a lady. Second, there is the all-pervading conviction that men, if not restrained by the formalities of a tacitly approved double standard (which sells them lesser and darker sex objects at the price of overt respect for ladies), will prove to be no gentlemen; that they will at the very least try to blacken the lady's name and with it her claim to a socially superior husband, or to the prospect of having her children marry upward. But there is also the equally ambivalent implication that any man who does not proceed to shed his gentleman's exterior when the opportunity offers itself is a weakling who only deserves to be mercilessly provoked. The usual feelings of guilt and inferiority all exist within the coordinates of a life plan which is dominated by the conscious hope for higher social status, and made morbid by its ambivalent counterpart, the hidden hope for the man who will dissolve the woman's need to be a lady in a moment of reckless passion. In all this there is a basic inability to conceive of any area in life where the standards and the words of a man and a woman could in honesty coincide and be lifted above a certain primeval antagonism. Needless to say, such unconscious standards cause severe suffering in sincere and enlightened women. But only the verbalization of these historical trends, concomitantly with the initial analysis of the patient's character resistances, makes psychoanalysis possible.

Psychoanalysts, in their daily work, are consulted by those who cannot stand the tension between polarities, the never-ceasing necessity of remaining tentative in order to be free to take the next step, to turn the next corner. These patients repeat in their transferences and in their resistances abortive attempts at synchronizing fast-changing and sharply contrasting remnants of national, regional, and class identities during critical stages of their childhood. The patient weaves the analyst into his unconscious life plan: he idealizes him (especially if he is European-born) by identifying him with his more homogeneous ancestors; or he subtly resists him as the enemy of a brittle and tentative ego identity.

The cured patient has the courage to face the discontinuities of life in this country and the polarities of its struggle for an economic and cultural identity, not as an imposed hostile reality, but as a potential promise for a more universal collective identity.

This finds its limits, however, where people are fundamentally impoverished in their childhood sensuality and stalled in their freedom to use opportunities.

In the experiences of pregenital stages the human infant learns the basic variables of organismic-social existence, before his libido becomes free for its procreative task. Child training, in creating a particular ratio of emphasis on such organismic modes as incorporation, retention, assimilation, elimination, intrusion and inclusion, gives the growing being a character basis suited to the main modes of later life tasks; if—indeed—later life tasks and early training are synchronized.

Consider our colored countrymen. Their babies often receive sensual satisfactions of oral and sensory surplus, adequate for a lifetime. It is preserved in the way in which they move, laugh, talk, sing. Their forced symbiosis with the feudal South capitalized on his oral-sensory treasure to build up a slave's identity: mild, submissive, dependent, somewhat querulous, but always ready to serve, and with occasional empathy and childlike wisdom. But underneath, a dangerous split occurred. The humiliating symbiosis on the one hand and, on the other, the necessity of the master race to protect its identity against sensual and oral temptations established in both groups an association: light—clean—clever—white; and, dark—dirty—dumb—nigger. The result, especially in those Negroes who have left the poor haven of their Southern homes, is often a violently sudden and cruel cleanliness training. This, in turn, transmits itself to the phallic-locomotor stage, in which the restrictions as to what shade of girl one may dream of and where one may move and act with abandon interfere at every moment of waking and dreaming with the free transfer of the original narcissistic sensuality to the genital sphere. Three identities are formed: (1) mammy's oral-sensual "honey child": tender, expressive, rhythmical; (2) the clean anal-compulsive, restrained, friendly, but always sad "white man's Negro"; and (3) the evil identity of the dirty, anal-sadistic, phallic-rapist "nigger."

When faced with so-called opportunities which only offer a

newly restricted freedom but fail to provide an integration of the identity fragments mentioned, one of these fragments becomes dominant in the form of a racial caricature; tired of this caricature, the colored individual often retires into hypochondriac invalidism as a condition which represents an analogy to the ego-space-time of defined restriction in the South: a neurotic regression to the ego identity of the slave.

I know of a colored boy who, like our boys, listens every night to the Lone Ranger. Then he sits up in bed, dreaming that he is the Ranger. But alas, the moment always comes when he sees himself galloping after some masked offenders and suddenly notices that in his image the Lone Ranger is a Negro. He stops his fantasies. While a child, this boy was extremely expressive, both in his pleasure and in his sorrows. Today he is calm and always smiles; his language is soft and blurred; nobody can hurry him, or worry him, or please him. White men like him.

EGO STRENGTH AND SOCIAL PATHOLOGY

1

Individual psychopathology contributes to the understanding of ego identity the study of its impairments by constitutional deficiency, early emotional impoverishment, neurotic conflict, and traumatic damage. Before we turn to examples of ego-damaging social pathology we may at least state a question, although its answer will have to wait for a more systematic presentation: what factors make for a strong normal ego identity? In a general way it is plain that everything that makes for a strong ego contributes to its identity.

Freud originally stated (1914) that the sources of human self-esteem (and thus an important infantile contribution to an individual's ego identity) are

1. the residue of infantile narcissism,
2. such infantile omnipotence as experience corroborates (the fulfillment of the ego ideal),
3. gratification of object libido.

Psychoanalysis came to emphasize the individual and regressive rather than the collective-supportive aspects of these statements. It was concerned with only half the story.

For if a residue of infantile narcissism is to survive, the maternal environment must create and sustain it with a love which assures the child that it is good to be alive in the particular social coordinates in which he happens to find himself. Infantile narcissism, which is said to fight so valiantly against the inroads of a frustrating environment, is in fact nourished by the sensual enrichment and the encouragement provided by this same environment. Widespread severe impoverishment of infantile narcissism (and thus of the basis of a strong ego) is lastly to be considered a breakdown of that collective synthesis which gives every newborn baby and his motherly surroundings a superindividual status as a trust of the community. In the later abandonment or transformation of this narcissism into more mature self-esteem, it is again of decisive importance whether or not the more realistic being can expect an opportunity to employ what he has learned and to acquire a feeling of increased communal meaning.

If experience is to corroborate part of the infantile sense of omnipotence, then child training must know not only how to teach sensual health and progressive mastery, but also how to offer tangible social recognition as the fruits of health and mastery. For unlike the infantile sense of omnipotence which is fed by make-believe and adult deception, the self-esteem attached to the ego identity is based on the rudiments of skills and social techniques which assure a gradual coincidence of functional pleasure and actual performance, of ego ideal and social role. The self-esteem attached to the ego identity contains the recognition of a tangible future.

If "object libido" is to be satisfied, then genital love and orgastic potency must be assured of a cultural synthesis of economic safety and emotional security; for only such a synthesis gives unified meaning to the full functional cycle of genitality, which includes conception, childbearing, and child rearing. Infatuation may project all the incestuous childhood loves into a present "object"; genital activity may help two individuals to use one another as an anchor against regression; but mutual genital love faces toward the future. It works toward a division of labor in that life task which only two of the opposite sex can fulfill together: the synthesis of production, procreation, and recreation in the primary social unit of the family. In this sense, then, ego identity acquires its final strength in the meeting of mates whose ego identity is complementary in some essential point and can be fused in marriage without the creation either of a dangerous discontinuity of tradition, or of an incestuous sameness—both of which are apt to prejudice the offspring's ego development.

The unconscious "incestuous" choice of a mate who resembles infantile love objects in some decisive feature is not to be considered as necessarily pathogenic, as writers in psychopathology seem to infer. Such a choice follows an ethnic mechanism in that it creates a continuity between the family one grew up in and the family one establishes: it thus perpetuates tradition, i.e., the sum of all that had been learned by preceding generations, in analogy to the preservation of the gains of evolution in the mating within the species. Neurotic fixation (and rigid inner defense against it) signifies the failure, not the nature, of this mechanism.

However, many of the mechanisms of adjustment which once made for evolutionary adaptation, tribal integration, national or class coherence, are at loose ends in a world of universally expanding identities. Education for an ego identity which receives strength from changing historical conditions demands a conscious acceptance of historical heterogeneity on the part of adults, combined with an enlightened effort to provide human childhood anywhere with a new fund of meaningful continuity. For this task, the systematic investigation of the following strategic points seems indicated:

1. The coherence of the body image, and its possible basis in fetal experience, with special reference to the importance of the mother's emotional attitude toward pregnancy.
2. The synchronization of the postnatal care with the newborn's temperament, based as it is on his prenatal and his birth experience.
3. The sameness and continuity of the early sensual experience of the mother's body and temperament, which nourishes and preserves a lasting fund of narcissism.
4. The synchronization of the pregenital stages and of the normative steps in child development with a group identity.
5. The immediate promise of tangible social recognition for the abandonment of infantile narcissism and autoerotism and for the acquisition of skills and knowledge during latency.
6. The adequacy of the solution of the oedipus conflict, within the individual's sociohistorical setting.
7. The relation of the final adolescent version of the ego identity to economic opportunities, realizable ideals, and available techniques.
8. The relation of genitality to love objects with complementary ego identities, and to the communal meaning of procreation.

2

What has already been said concerning the collective space-time and the life plan of a society shows the necessity of studying the spontaneous ways in which segments of modern society strive to make a workable continuity out of child training and economic development. For whoever wants to guide, must understand, conceptualize, and use spontaneous trends of identity formation. Our clinical histories help in such research, where they avoid being too episodic in type, and where stereotypes, such as "the patient had a domineering mother" (which are based on comparisons with a family image implied in classical European psychiatry) are further broken down into historically significant variations. During World War II, psychiatric and psychoanalytic attempts at explaining what childhood milieus cause or do not cause a man to break down under military stress on the whole failed for lack of historical perspective.

In our work with veterans discharged from the armed forces as psychoneurotics before the end of hostilities, we became familiar with the universal symptoms of partial loss of ego synthesis. Many of these men, indeed, regress to the "stage of unlearned function" (Freud, 1908). The boundaries of their egos have lost their shock-absorbing delineation: anxiety and anger are provoked by everything too sudden or too intense, whether it be a sensory impression or a self-reproach, an impulse or a memory. A ceaselessly "startled" sensory system is attacked by stimuli from outside as well as by somatic sensations: heat flashes, palpitation, cutting headaches. Insomnia hinders the nightly restoration of sensory screening by sleep, and that of emotional synthesis by dreaming. Amnesia, neurotic pseudologia, and confusion show the partial loss of time-binding and of spatial orientation. What definable symptoms and remnants of "peacetime neuroses" there are have a fragmentary and false quality, as if the ego could not even accomplish an organized neurosis.

In some cases this ego impairment seems to have its origin in violent events, in others in the gradual grind of a million annoyances. Obviously the men are worn out by too many changes (gradual or sudden) in too many respects at once; somatic tension, social panic, and ego anxiety are always present. Above all, the men "do not know any more who they are": there is a distinct loss of ego identity. The sense of sameness and of continuity and the belief in one's social role are gone.

The American group identity supports an individual's ego identity as long as he can preserve a certain element of deliberate tentativeness, as long as he can convince himself that the next step is up to him and that no matter where he is staying or going he always has the choice of leaving or turning in the opposite direction if he chooses to do so. In this country the migrant does not want to be told to move on, nor the sedentary man to stay where he is; for the life style of each contains the opposite element as an alternate which he wishes to consider his most private and individual decision. For many men, then, the restraint and discipline of army life provides few ideal prototypes.[9] To quite a few, it represents instead the intensely evil identity of the sucker; one who lets himself be sidetracked, cooped up, and stalled, while others are free to pursue his chance and his girl. But to be a sucker means to be a social and sexual castrate; if you are a sucker, not even a mother's pity will be with you.

In the (often profuse) utterances of psychoneurotic casualties, all those memories and anticipations appear associated that ever threatened or are expected to threaten the freedom of the next step. In their struggle to regain access to the nonreversible escalator of free enterprise, their traumatized ego fights and flees an evil identity which includes elements of the crying baby, the bleeding woman, the submissive nigger, the sexual sissy, the economic sucker, the mental moron—all prototypes the mere allusion to which can bring these men close to homicidal or suicidal rage, ending up in varying degrees of irritability or apathy. Their exaggerated attempt to blame their ego dilemma on circumstances and individuals gives their childhood history a more sordid character and themselves the appearance of a worse psychopathy than is justified. Their ego identity has fallen apart into its bodily, sexual, social, occupational elements, each having to overcome again the danger of its evil prototype. Rehabilitation work can be made more effective and economical if the clinical investigation focuses on the patient's shattered life plan and if advice tends to strengthen the resynthesis of the elements on which the patient's ego identity was based.

In addition to the several hundred thousand men who lost and only gradually or partially regained their ego identity in this war and to the thousands whose acute loss of ego identity was falsely diagnosed and treated as psychopathy, an untold number has experienced to the core the threat of a traumatic loss of ego identity as a result of radical historical change.

The fact that these men, their physicians, and their contemporaries in increasing numbers turn to the bitter truths of psychoanalytic psychiatry is in itself a historical development which calls for critical appraisal. It expresses an increased acceptance of psychoanalytic insights in so far as they concern the meaning of anxiety and of disease in the individual case history. Yet this partial acceptance of painful unconscious determinants of human behavior has the quality of a concomitant resistance against the disquieting awareness of a social symptom and its historical determinants. I mean the subliminal panic which accompanied the large-scale testing of the American identity during the most recent period of world history.

Historical change has reached a coercive universality and a global acceleration which is experienced as a threat to the emerging American identity. It seems to devaluate the vigorous conviction that this nation can afford mistakes; that this nation, by definition, is always so far ahead of the rest of the world in inexhaustible reserves, in vision of planning, in freedom of action, and in tempo of progress that there is unlimited space and endless time in which to develop, to test, and to complete her social experiments. The difficulties met in the attempt to integrate this old image of insulated spaciousness with the new image of explosive global closeness are deeply disquieting. They are characteristically met, at first, with the application of traditional methods to a new space-time; there is the missionary discovery of "One World," aviation pioneering on a "Trans-World" basis, charity on a global scale, etc. Yet there also remains a deep consciousness of a lag in economic and political integration, and with it, in emotional and spiritual strength.

The psychotherapist, in disregarding the contribution of this development to neurotic discomfort, is apt not only to miss much of the specific dynamics in contemporary life cycles; he is apt also to deflect (or to serve those whose business demands that they deflect) individual energy from the collective tasks at hand. A large-scale decrease of neurosis can be achieved only by equal clinical attention to cases and to conditions, to the fixation on the past and the emerging design for the future, to the grumbling depth and the unsafe surface.

3

In studying the ego's relation to changing historical reality, psychoanalysis approaches a new phalanx of unconscious resistances. It is implicit in the nature of psychoanalytic investigation that such resistances must be located and appraised in the observer, and in his habits of conceptualization, before their presence in the observed can be fully understood and effectively handled. When investigating instincts, the psychoanalyst knows that his drive to investigate is partially instinctive in nature; he knows that he responds with a partial countertransference to the patient's transference, i.e., the ambiguous wish to satisfy infantile strivings in the very therapeutic situation which is to cure them. The analyst acknowledges all this, yet works methodically toward that margin of freedom where the clear delineation of the inevitable makes consuming resistances unnecessary and frees energy for creative planning.

It is, then, a commonplace to state that the psychoanalyst in training must learn to study the historical determinants of what made him what he is before he can hope to perfect that human gift: the ability to understand what is different from him. Beyond this, however, there are the historical determinants of psychoanalytic concepts.

If in the field of human motivation, the same terms have been used over a period of half a century (and what a century!), they cannot but reflect the ideologies of their day of origin and absorb the connotations of consequent social changes. Ideological connotation is historically inevitable in the use of conceptual tools which concern the ego, man's organ of reality testing. The conceptualizations of man's selfsame core and of reality itself are by necessity a function of historical change. Yet, here too, our search is for a margin of freedom; our method, radical analysis of resistances to insight and to planning.

As philosophers would predict, the concept of "reality" itself, while clear in its intended meaning, is highly corruptible in its usage. According to the pleasure principle, that is good which feels good at the moment; the reality principle declares that to be good which in the long run and with consideration for all possible outer and inner developments promises most lastingly to feel good. Such principles, established by scientific man, fall prey easily to economic man. The reality principle, in theory and therapy, has taken on a certain individualistic color, according to which that is good which the individual can get away with by dodging the law (in so far as it happens to be enforced) and the superego (in so far as it causes discomfort). Our therapeutic failures often define the limit of this usage: Western man, almost against his will, is developing a more universal group identity. His reality principle begins to include a *social principle* according to which that is good which, in the long run, secures to a man what feels good to him without keeping any other man (of the same collective identity) from securing an analogous gain. The question that remains is: what new synthesis of economic and emotional safety will sustain this wider group identity and thus give strength to the individual ego?

A different sort of trend in contemporary conceptualization is typified in a recent formulation, according to which "all through childhood a maturation process is at work which, in the service of an increasing knowledge and adaptation to reality, aims at perfecting [ego] functions, at rendering them more and more objective and independent of the emotions until they can become as accurate and reliable as a mechanical apparatus" (Anna Freud, 1945).

Obviously, the ego as such is older than all mechanization. If we detect in it a tendency to mechanize itself and to be free from the very emotions without which experience becomes impoverished, we may actually be concerned with a historical dilemma. Today we face the question whether the problems of the machine age will be solved by a mechanization of man or by a humanization of industry. Our child-training customs have begun to standardize modern man, so that he may become a reliable mechanism prepared to "adjust" to the competitive exploitation of the machine world. In fact, certain modern trends in child training seem to represent a magic identification with the machine, analogous to identifications of primitive tribes with their principal prey. At the same time the modern mind, already the product of a civilization preoccupied with mechanization, attempts to understand itself by searching for "mental mechanisms." If, then, the ego itself seems to *crave* mechanical-adaptation we may not be dealing with the nature of the ego, but with one of its period-bound adjustments as well as with our own mechanistic approach to its study.

Maybe in this connection it is not quite unnecessary to point to the fact that the popular use of the word "ego" in this country has, of course, little to do with the psychoanalytic concept of the same name; it denotes unqualified if not justified self-esteem. Yet, in the wake of therapeutic short cuts, this connotation can be seen to creep even into professional discussions of the ego.

Bolstering, bantering, boisterousness, and other "ego-inflating" behavior is, of course, part of the American folkways. As such, it pervades speech and gesture and enters into all interpersonal relations. Without it, a therapeutic relationship in this country would remain outlandish and nonspecific. The problem to be discussed here, however, is the systematic exploitation of the national practice of bolstering for the sake of making people "feel better," or of submerging their anxiety and tension so as to make them function better as patients, customers, or employees.

A weak ego does not gain substantial strength from being persistently bolstered. A strong ego, secured in its identity by a strong society, does not need, and in fact is immune to any attempt at artificial inflation. Its tendency is toward the testing of what feels real; the mastery of that which works; the understanding of that which proves necessary, the enjoyment of the vital, and extermination of the morbid. At the same time, it tends toward the creation of a strong mutual reinforcement with others in a group ego, which will transmit its will to the next generation.

A war, however, can be an unfair test to ego strength. During collective emergencies all resources, emotional as well as material, must be mobilized with relative disregard for what is workable and economical under more normal conditions of long-range development. Ego bolstering is a legitimate measure in such days of collective danger; and it remains a genuine therapeutic approach in individual cases of acute ego strain, i.e., wherever the individual is emotionally too young or physically too weak to meet a situation bearable to the mature and the healthy; or if a situation is too extraordinary to be met even by a relatively adequate ego. Obviously, a war increases the occurrence of both types of traumatic discrepancy between the ego and situations not included in its anticipations. The indiscriminate application of the philosophy and the practice of "ego bolstering" to peacetime conditions, however, would be theoretically unsound and therapeutically unwholesome. It is, furthermore, socially dangerous, because its employment implies that the cause of the strain (i.e., "modern living") is perpetually beyond the individual's or his society's control—a state of affairs which would postpone indefinitely the revision of *conditions which are apt to weaken the infantile ego*. To deflect energy from such revision is dangerous. For American childhood and other manifestations of the specific American freedom of spirit are but grandiose fragments striving for integration with the fragments of industrial democracy.

The effectiveness of the psychoanalytic contribution to this development is guaranteed solely by the persistent humanistic intention, beyond the mere adjustment of patients to limited conditions, to apply clinical experience to the end of making man aware of potentialities which are clouded by archaic fear.

4

In studying his subject, the psychoanalyst (so Anna Freud [1936] points out) should occupy an observation point "equidistant from the id, the ego, and the superego"—so that he may be aware of their functional interdependence and so that, as he observes a change in one of these sections of the mind, he may not lose sight of related changes in the others.

Beyond this, however, the observer is aware of the fact that what he conceptualizes as id, ego, and superegos are not static compartments in the capsule of a life history. Rather they reflect three major processes the relativity of which determines the form of human behavior. They are

1. the process of organismic organization of bodies within the time-space of the life cycle (evolution, epigenesis, libido development, etc.),
2. the process of the organization of experience by ego synthesis (ego space-time, ego defenses, ego identity, etc.),
3. the process of the social organization of ego organisms in geographic-historical units (collective space-time, collective life plan, ethos of production, etc.).

The order given follows the trend of psychoanalytic research. Otherwise, although different in structure, these processes *exist by and are relative to each other*. Any item whose meaning and potential changes within one of these processes simultaneously changes in the others. To assure the proper rate and sequence of change, and to prevent or counteract lags, discrepancies, and discontinuities of development, there are the warning signals of pain in the body, anxiety in the ego, and panic in the group. They warn of organic dysfunction, impairment of ego mastery, and loss of group identity: each a threat to all.

In psychopathology we observe and study the apparent autonomy of one of these processes as it receives undue accentuation because of the loss of their mutual regulation and general balance. Thus psychoanalysis first studied (as if it could be isolated) man's *enslavement by the id*, i.e., by the excessive demands on ego and society of frustrated organisms, upset in the inner economy of their life cycle. Next the focus of study shifted to man's *enslavement by seemingly autonomous ego (and superego) strivings*—defensive mechanisms which curtail and distort the ego's power of experiencing and planning beyond the limit of what is workable and tolerable in the individual organism and in social organization. Psychoanalysis completes its basic studies of neurosis by investigating more explicitly *man's enslavement by historical conditions which claim autonomy* by precedent and exploit archaic mechanisms within him to deny him health and ego strength.[10] Only the reinterpretation of our clinical experience on the basis of this threefold investigation will permit us to make an essential contribution to child training in an industrial world.

The goal of psychoanalytic treatment itself has been defined (Nunberg, 1931) as a simultaneous increase in the mobility of the id, in the tolerance of the superego, and in the synthesizing power of the ego. To the last point we add the suggestion that the analysis of the ego should include that of the individual's ego identity in relation to the historical changes which dominated his childhood milieu. For the individual's mastery over his neurosis begins where he is put in a position to accept the historical necessity which made him what he is. The individual feels free when he can choose to identify with his own ego identity and when he learns to apply that which is given to that which must be done. Only thus can he derive ego strength (for his generation and the next) from the coincidence of his one and only life cycle with a particular segment of human history.

2

Growth and Crises
of the
Healthy Personality

THE FACT-FINDING COMMITTEE of the White House Conference
on Childhood and Youth has asked me to repeat here in greater
detail a few ideas set forth in another context (Erikson, 1950a).
There the matter of the healthy personality emerges, as if accidentally, from a variety of clinical and anthropological considerations. Here it is to become the central theme.

An expert, it is said, can separate fact from theory, and knowledge from opinion. It is his job to know the available techniques
by which statements in his field can be verified. If, in this paper, I
were to restrict myself to what is, in this sense, *known* about the
"healthy personality," I would lead the reader and myself into a
very honorable but very uninspiring austerity. In the matter of
man's relation to himself and to others, methodological problems

The original version of this paper appeared in *Symposium on the Healthy Personality*, Supplement II; Problems of Infancy and Childhood, Transactions of Fourth Conference, March,
1950, M. J. E. Senn, ed. New York: Josiah Macy, Jr. Foundation.

are not such as to be either instructive or suggestive in a short treatise.

On the other hand, if I were to write this paper in order to give another introduction to the theory of Freudian psychoanalysis, I would hardly contribute much to an understanding of the healthy personality. For the psychoanalyst knows very much more about the dynamics and cure of the disturbances which he treats daily than about the prevention of such disturbances.

I will, however, start out from Freud's far-reaching discovery that neurotic conflict is not very different in content from the conflicts which every child must live through in his childhood, and that every adult carries these conflicts with him in the recesses of his personality. I shall take account of this fact by stating for each childhood stage what these critical psychological conflicts are. For man, to remain psychologically alive, must resolve these conflicts unceasingly, even as his body must unceasingly combat the encroachment of physical decomposition. However, since I cannot accept the conclusion that just to be alive, or not to be sick, means to be healthy, I must have recourse to a few concepts which are not part of the official terminology of my field. Being interested also in cultural anthropology, I shall try to describe those elements of a really healthy personality which—so it seems to me—are most noticeably absent or defective in neurotic patients and which are most obviously present in the kind of man that educational and cultural systems seem to be striving, each in its own way, to create, to support, and to maintain.

I shall present human growth from the point of view of the conflicts, inner and outer, which the healthy personality weathers, emerging and re-emerging with an increased sense of inner unity, with an increase of good judgment, and an increase in the capacity to do well, according to the standards of those who are significant to him. The use of the words "to do well," of course, points up the whole question of cultural relativity. For example, those who are significant to a man may think he is doing well when he "does some good"; or when he "does well" in the sense of acquiring possessions; or when he is doing well in the sense of learning new skills or new ways of understanding or mastering reality; or when he is not much more than just getting along.

Formulations of what constitutes a healthy personality in an adult are presented in other parts of the Fact-finding Committee's work. If I may take up only one, namely, Marie Jahoda's (1950) definition, according to which a healthy personality *actively masters his environment*, shows a certain *unity of personality*, and is able to *perceive the world and himself correctly*, it is clear that all of these criteria are relative to the child's cognitive and social development. In fact, we may say that childhood is defined by their initial absence and by their gradual development in many complicated steps. I consider it my task to approach this question from the genetic point of view: How does a healthy personality grow or, as it were, accrue from the successive stages of increasing capacity to master life's outer and inner dangers—with some vital enthusiasm to spare?

ON HEALTH AND GROWTH

Whenever we try to understand growth, it is well to remember the *epigenetic principle* which is derived from the growth of organisms *in utero*. Somewhat generalized, this principle states that anything that grows has a *ground plan,* and that out of this ground plan the *parts* arise, each part having its *time* of special ascendancy, until all parts have arisen to form a *functioning whole.* At birth the baby leaves the chemical exchange of the womb for the social exchange system of his society, where his gradually increasing capacities meet the opportunities and limitations of his culture. How the maturing organism continues to unfold, not by developing new organs, but by a prescribed sequence of locomotor, sensory, and social capacities, is described in the child-development literature. Psychoanalysis has given us an understanding of the more idiosyncratic experiences and especially the inner conflicts, which constitute the manner in which an individual becomes a distinct personality. But here, too, it is important to realize that in the sequence of his most personal experiences the healthy child, given a reasonable amount of guidance, can be trusted to obey inner laws of development, laws which create a *succession of potentialities for significant interaction* with those who tend him. While such interaction varies from culture to culture, it must remain within the *proper rate and the proper sequence* which govern the *growth of a personality* as well as that of an organism. Personality can be said to develop according to steps predetermined in the human organism's readiness to be driven toward, to be aware of, and to interact with, a widening social radius, beginning with the dim image of a mother and ending with mankind, or at any rate that segment of mankind which "counts" in the particular individual's life.

It is for this reason that, in the presentation of stages in the development of the personality, we employ an *epigenetic diagram* analogous to one previously employed for an analysis of Freud's psychosexual stages.[1] It is, in fact, the purpose of this presentation to bridge the theory of infantile sexuality (without repeating it here in detail) and our knowledge of the child's physical and social growth within his family and the social structure. An epigenetic diagram is as shown in Figure I.

The double-lined squares signify both a sequence of stages (I to III) and a gradual development of component parts; in other words the diagram formalizes a *progression through time of a differentiation of parts.* This indicates (1) that each item of the healthy personality to be discussed is *systematically related to all others*, and that they all depend on the *proper development in the proper sequence of each item;* and (2) that each item *exists in some form before "its" decisive and critical time* normally arrives.

If I say, for example, that a *sense of basic trust* is the first component of mental health to develop in life, a *sense of autonomous will* the second, and a *sense of initiative* the third, the purpose of the diagram may become clearer (see Figure II).

This diagrammatic statement, in turn, is meant to express a

	Component 1	Component 2	Component 3
Stage I	I₁	I₂	I₃
Stage II	II₁	II₂	II₃
Stage III	III₁	III₂	III₃

Figure I

	Component 1	Component 2	Component 3
First Stage (about first year)	BASIC TRUST	Earlier form of AUTONOMY	Earlier form of INITIATIVE
Second Stage (about second and third years)	Later form of BASIC TRUST	AUTONOMY	Earlier form of INITIATIVE
Third State (about fourth and fifth years)	Later form of BASIC TRUST	Later form of AUTONOMY	INITIATIVE

Figure II

number of fundamental relations that exist among the three components, as well as a few fundamental facts for each.

Each comes to its ascendance, meets its crisis, and finds its lasting solution (in ways to be described here) *toward the end of the stages* mentioned. All of them exist in the beginning in some form, although we do not make a point of this fact, and we shall not confuse things by calling these components different names at earlier or later stages. A baby may show something like "autonomy" from the beginning, for example, in the particular way in which he angrily tries to wriggle his hand free when tightly held. However, under normal conditions, it is not until the second year that he begins to experience the whole *critical alternative between being an autonomous creature and being a dependent one;* and it is not until then that he is ready for a *decisive encounter* with his environment, an environment which, in turn, feels called upon to convey to him its *particular ideas and concepts of autonomy and coercion* in ways decisively contributing to the character, the efficiency, and the health of his personality in his culture.

It is this *encounter*, together with the resulting crisis, which is to be described for each stage. Each stage becomes a *crisis* because incipient growth and awareness in a significant part function goes together with a shift in instinctual energy and yet causes specific vulnerability in that part. One of the most difficult questions to decide, therefore, is whether or not a child at a given stage is weak or strong. Perhaps it would be best to say that he is always vulnerable in some respects and completely oblivious and insensitive in others, but that at the same time he is unbelievably persistent in the same respects in which he is vulnerable. It must be added that the smallest baby's weakness gives him power; out of his very dependence and weakness he makes signs to which his environment (if it is guided well by a responsiveness based both on instinctive and traditional patterns) is peculiarly sensitive. A baby's presence exerts a consistent and persistent domination over the outer and inner lives of every member of a household. Because these members must reorient themselves to accommodate his presence, they must also grow as individuals and as a group. It is as true to say that babies control and bring up their families as it is to say the converse. A family can bring up a baby only by being brought up by him. His growth consists of a series of challenges to them to serve his newly developing potentialities for social interaction.

Each successive step, then, is a potential crisis because of a radical *change in perspective.* There is, at the beginning of life, the most radical change of all: from intrauterine to extrauterine life. But in postnatal existence, too, such radical adjustments of perspective as lying relaxed, sitting firmly, and running fast must all be accomplished in their own good time. With them, the interpersonal perspective, too, changes rapidly and often radically, as is testified by the proximity in time of such opposites as "not letting mother out of sight" and "wanting to be independent." Thus, *different capacities use different opportunities* to become full-grown components of the ever-new configuration that is the growing personality.

BASIC TRUST VERSUS BASIC MISTRUST

1

For the first component of a healthy personality I nominate a sense of *basic trust*, which I think is an attitude toward oneself and the world derived from the experiences of the first year of life. By "trust" I mean what is commonly implied in reasonable trustfulness as far as others are concerned and a simple sense of trustworthiness as far as oneself is concerned. When I say "basic," I mean that neither this component nor any of those that follow are, either in childhood or in adulthood, especially conscious. In fact, all of these criteria, when developed in childhood and when integrated in adulthood, blend into the total personality. Their crises in childhood, however, and their impairment in adulthood are clearly circumscribed.

In describing this growth and its crises as a development of a series of alternative basic attitudes, we take recourse to the term *"a sense of."* Like a "sense of health" or a "sense of not being well," such "senses" pervade surface and depth, consciousness and the unconscious. They are ways of conscious *experience*, accessible to introspection (where it develops); ways of *behaving*, observable by others; and unconscious *inner states* determinable by test and analysis. It is important to keep these three dimensions in mind, as we proceed.

In *adults* the impairment of basic trust is expressed in a *basic mistrust*. It characterizes individuals who withdraw into themselves in particular ways when at odds with themselves and with others. These ways, which often are not obvious, are more strikingly represented by individuals who regress into psychotic states in which they sometimes close up, refusing food and comfort and becoming oblivious to companionship. In so far as we hope to assist them with psychotherapy, we must try to reach them again in specific ways in order to convince them that they can trust the world and that they can trust themselves (Fromm-Reichmann, 1950).

It is from the knowledge of such radical regressions and of the deepest and most infantile layers in our not-so-sick patients that we have learned to regard basic trust as the cornerstone of a healthy personality. Let us see what justifies our placing the crisis and the ascendancy of this component at the beginning of life.

As the newborn infant is separated from his symbiosis with the mother's body, his inborn and more or less coordinated ability to take in by mouth meets the mother's more or less coordinated ability and intention to feed him and to welcome him. At this point he lives through, and loves with, his mouth; and the mother lives through, and loves with, her breasts.

For the mother this is a late and complicated accomplishment, highly dependent on her development as a woman, on her unconscious attitude toward the child, on the way she has lived through pregnancy and delivery, on her and her community's attitude toward the act of nursing—and on the response of the newborn. To him the mouth is the focus of a general first approach to life—the *incorporative* approach. In psychoanalysis this stage is usually referred to as the "oral" stage. Yet it is clear that, in addition to the overwhelming need for food, a baby is, or soon becomes, receptive in many other respects. As he is willing and able to suck on appropriate objects and to swallow whatever appropriate fluids they emit, he is soon also willing and able to "take in" with his eyes whatever enters his visual field. His tactual senses, too, seem to "take in" what feels good. In this sense, then, one could speak of an "*incorporative stage*," one in which he is, relatively speaking, receptive to what he is being offered. Yet many babies are sensitive and vulnerable, too. In order to ensure that their first experience in this world may not only keep them alive but also help them to coordinate their sensitive breathing and their metabolic and circulatory rhythms, we must see to it that we deliver to their senses stimuli as well as food in the proper intensity and at the right time; otherwise their willingness to accept may change abruptly into diffuse defense—or into lethargy.

Now, while it is quite clear what *must* happen to keep a baby alive (the minimum supply necessary) and what *must not* happen, lest he be physically damaged or chronically upset (the maximum early frustration tolerable), there is a certain leeway in regard to what *may* happen; and different cultures make extensive use of their prerogatives to decide what they consider workable and insist upon calling necessary. Some people think that a baby, lest he scratch his own eyes out, must necessarily be swaddled completely for the better part of the day and throughout the greater part of the first year; also, that he should be rocked or fed whenever he whimpers. Others think that he should feel the freedom of his kicking limbs as early as possible, but also that he, as a matter of course, be forced to cry "please" for his meals until he literally gets blue in the face. All of this (more or less consciously) seems related to the culture's general aim and system. I have known some old American Indians who bitterly decried the way in which we often let our small babies cry because we believe that "it will make their lungs strong." No wonder (these Indians said) that the white man, after such an initial reception, seems to be in a hurry to get to the "next world." But the same Indians spoke proudly of the way their infants (breast fed into the second year) became blue in the face with fury when thumped on the head for "biting" the mother's nipples; here the Indians, in turn, believed that "it's going to make good hunters of them."

There is some intrinsic wisdom, some unconscious planning and much superstition in the seemingly arbitrary varieties of child training: what is "good for the child," what *may* happen to him, depends on what he is supposed to become and where.

At any rate, it is already in his earliest encounters that the human infant meets up with the basic modalities of his culture. The simplest and the earliest modality is *"to get,"* not in the sense of *"go and get"* but in that of receiving and accepting what is given; and this sounds easier than it is. For the groping and unstable newborn's organism learns this modality only as he learns to regulate his readiness to get with the methods of a mother who, in turn, will permit him to coordinate his means of getting as she develops and coordinates her means of giving. The mutuality of relaxation thus developed is of prime importance for the first experience of friendly otherness: from psychoanalysis one receives the impression that in thus *getting what is given,* and in learning to *get somebody to do* for him what he wishes to have done, the baby also develops the necessary groundwork to *get to be* the giver, to "identify" with her.

Where this *mutual regulation* fails, the situation falls apart into a variety of attempts to control by duress rather than by reciprocity. The baby will try to get by random activity what he cannot get by central suction; he will activate himself into exhaustion or he will find his thumb and damn the world. The mother's reaction may be to try to control matters by nervously changing hours, formulas, and procedures. One cannot be sure what this does to a baby; but it certainly is our clinical impression that in some sensitive individuals (or in individuals whose early frustration was never compensated for) such a situation can be a model for a radical disturbance in their relationship to the "world," to "people," and especially to loved or otherwise significant people.

There are ways of maintaining reciprocity by giving to the baby what he can get through other forms of feeding and by making up for what is missed orally through the satiation of other than oral receptors: his pleasure in being held, warmed, smiled at, talked to, rocked, and so forth. Besides such *"horizontal" compensation* (compensation during the same stage of development) there are many *"longitudinal" compensations* in life: compensations emerging from later stages of the life cycle.[2]

During the "second oral" stage the ability and the pleasure in a more active and more directed incorporative approach ripen. The teeth develop and with them the pleasure in biting *on* hard things, in biting *through* things, and in biting *off* things. This *active-incorporative* mode characterizes a variety of other activities (as did the first incorporative mode). The eyes, first part of a passive system of accepting impressions as they come along, have now learned to focus, to isolate, to "grasp" objects from the vaguer background and to follow them. The organs of hearing similarly have learned to discern significant sounds, to localize them, and to guide an appropriate change in position (lifting and turning the head, lifting and turning the upper body). The arms have learned to reach out determinedly and the hands to grasp firmly. We are more interested here in the over-all *configuration and final integration* of developing approaches to the world than in the *first appearance of specific abilities* which are so well described in the child-development literature.[3]

With all of this a number of interpersonal patterns are established which center in the social modality of *taking* and *holding on to* things—things which are more or less freely offered and given, and things which have more or less a tendency to slip away. As the baby learns to change positions, to roll over, and very gradually to establish himself on the throne of his sedentary kingdom, he must perfect the mechanisms of grasping and appropriating, holding and chewing all that is within his reach.

The *crisis* of the oral stage (during the second part of the first year) is difficult to assess and more difficult to verify. It seems to consist of the coincidence in time of three developments: (1) a physiological one: the general tension associated with a more violent drive to incorporate, appropriate, and observe more actively (a tension to which is added the discomfort of "teething" and other changes in the oral machinery); (2) a psychological one: the infant's increasing awareness of himself as a distinct person; and (3) an environmental one: the mother's apparent turning away from the baby toward pursuits which she had given up during late pregnancy and postnatal care. These pursuits include her full return to conjugal intimacy and may soon lead to a new pregnancy.

Where breast feeding lasts into the biting stage (and, generally speaking, this has been the rule) it is now necessary to learn how to continue sucking without biting, so that the mother may not withdraw the nipple in pain or anger. Our clinical work indicates that this point in the individual's early history provides him with some sense of basic loss, leaving the general impression that once upon a time one's unity with a maternal matrix was destroyed. Weaning, therefore, should not mean sudden loss of the breast and loss of the mother's reassuring presence too, unless, of course, other women can be depended upon to sound and feel much like the mother. A drastic loss of accustomed mother love without proper substitution at this time can lead (under otherwise aggravating conditions) to acute infantile depression (Spitz, 1945) or to a mild but chronic state of mourning which may give a depressive undertone to the whole remainder of life. But even under more favorable circumstances, this stage seems to introduce into the psychic life a sense of division and a dim but universal nostalgia for a lost paradise.

It is against the combination of these impressions of having been deprived, of having been divided, and of having been abandoned, all of which leave a residue of basic mistrust, that basic trust must be established and maintained.[4]

2

What we here call "trust" coincides with what Therese Benedek has called "confidence." If I prefer the word "trust," it is because there is more naïveté and more mutuality in it: an infant can be said to be trusting, but it would be assuming too much to say that he "has confidence." The general state of trust, furthermore, implies not only that one has learned to rely on the sameness and continuity of the outer providers but also that one may trust oneself and the capacity of one's own organs to cope with urges; that one is able to consider oneself trustworthy enough so that the providers will not need to be on guard or to leave.

In the psychiatric literature we find frequent references to an "oral character," which is a characterological deviation based on the unsolved conflicts of this stage. Wherever oral pessimism becomes dominant and exclusive, infantile fears, such as that of "being left empty," or simply of "being left," and also of being "starved of stimulation," can be discerned in the depressive forms of "being empty" and of "being no good." Such fears, in turn, can give orality that particular avaricious quality which in psychoanalysis is called "oral sadism," that is, a cruel need to get and to take in ways harmful to others. But there is an optimistic oral character, too, one which has learned to make giving and receiving the most important thing in life; and there is "orality" as a normal substratum in all individuals, a lasting residuum of this first period of dependency on powerful providers. It normally expresses itself in our dependencies and nostalgias, and in our all too hopeful and all too hopeless states. The integration of the oral stage with all the following ones results, in adulthood, in a combination of faith and realism.

The pathology and irrationality of oral trends depend entirely on the degree to which they are integrated with the rest of the personality and the degree to which they fit into the general cultural pattern and use approved interpersonal techniques for their expression.

Here, as elsewhere, we must therefore consider as a topic for discussion the expression of *infantile urges* in *cultural patterns* which one may (or may not) consider a pathological deviation in the total economic or moral system of a culture or a nation. One could speak, for example, of the invigorating belief in "chance," that traditional prerogative of American trust in one's own resourcefulness and in Fate's store of good intentions. This belief, at times, can be seen to degenerate—in large-scale gambling, or in "taking chances" in the form of an arbitrary and often suicidal provocation of Fate, or in the insistence that one has not only the right to an equal chance but also the privilege of being preferred over all other investors in the same general enterprise. In a similar way all the pleasant reassurances which can be derived (especially in good company) from old and new taste sensations, from inhaling and imbibing, from munching and swallowing and digesting, can turn into mass addictions neither expressive of, nor conducive to, the kind of basic trust which we have in mind.

Here we are obviously touching on phenomena the analysis of which would call for a comprehensive approach both to personality and to culture. This would be true also for an epidemiological approach to the problem of the more or less malignant elaboration of the oral character in "schizoid" characters and the mental diseases seemingly expressive of an underlying weakness in oral reassurance and basic trust. A related problem is the belief (reflected in much of contemporary obstetric and pediatric concern with the methods of child care) that the establishment of a basic sense of trust in earliest childhood makes adult individuals less dependent on mild or malignant forms of addiction, on self-delusion, and on avaricious appropriation.

At any rate, the psychiatrists, obstetricians, pediatricians, and anthropologists, to whom I feel closest, today would agree that the *firm establishment of enduring patterns for the balance of basic trust over basic mistrust* is the first task of the budding personality and therefore first of all a task for maternal care. But it must be said that the *amount of trust* derived from earliest infantile experience does not seem to depend on absolute *quantities of food or demonstrations of love* but rather on the *quality* of the maternal relationship. Mothers create a sense of trust in their children by that kind of administration which in its quality combines sensitive care of the baby's individual needs and a firm sense of personal trustworthiness within the trusted framework of their community's life style. (This forms the basis in the child for a sense of identity which will later combine a sense of being "all right," of being oneself, and of becoming what other people trust one will become.) Parents must not only have certain ways of guiding by prohibition and permission; they must also be able to represent to the child a deep, an almost somatic conviction that there is a meaning to what they are doing. In this sense a traditional system of child care can be said to be a factor making for trust, even where certain items of that tradition, taken singly, may seem irrational or unnecessarily cruel. Here much depends on whether such items are inflicted on the child by the parent in the firm traditional belief that this is the only way to do things or whether the parent misuses his administration of the baby and the child in order to work off anger, alleviate fear, or win an argument, with the child or with somebody else (mother-in-law, doctor, or priest).

In times of change—and what other times are there, in our memory?—one generation differs so much from another that items of tradition often become disturbances. Conflicts between mother's ways and one's own self-made ways, conflicts between the expert's advice and mother's ways, and conflicts between the expert's authority and one's own self-willed ways may disturb a mother's trust in herself. Furthermore, all the mass transformations in American life (immigration, migration, and Americanization; industrialization, urbanization, mechanization, and others) are apt to disturb young mothers in those tasks which are so simple yet so far-reaching. No wonder, then, that the first section of the first chapter of Benjamin Spock's (1945) book is entitled "Trust Yourself." But while it is true that the expert obstetrician and pediatrician can do much to replace the binding power of tradition by giving reassurance and guidance, he does not have the time to become the father-confessor for all the doubts and fears, angers and arguments, which can fill the minds of lonely young parents. Maybe a book like Spock's needs to be read in study groups where the true psychological spirit of the town meeting can be created; that is, where matters are considered to be agreed upon not because somebody said so, but because the free airing of opinions and emotions, of prejudices and of errors has led to a general area of relative consent and of tolerant good will.

This chapter has become unduly long. In regard to the matters discussed here, it is too bad that one must begin with the beginning. We know so little of the beginnings, of the deeper strata of the human mind. But since we have already embarked on general observations, a word must be said about one cultural and traditional institution which is deeply related to the matter of trust, namely, religion.

It is not the psychologist's job to decide whether religion should or should not be confessed and practiced in particular words and rituals. Rather the psychological observer must ask whether or not in any area under observation religion and tradition are living psychological forces creating the kind of faith and conviction which permeates a parent's personality and thus reinforces the child's basic trust in the world's trustworthiness. The psychopathologist cannot avoid observing that there are millions of people who cannot really afford to be without religion, and whose pride in not having it is that much whistling in the dark. On the other hand, there are millions who seem to derive faith from other than religious dogmas, that is, from fellowship, productive work, social action, scientific pursuit, and artistic creation. And again, there are millions who profess faith, yet in practice mistrust both life and man. With all of these in mind, it seems worth while to speculate on the fact that religion through the centuries has served to restore a sense of trust at regular intervals in the form of faith while giving tangible form to a sense of evil which it promises to ban. All religions have in common the periodical childlike surrender to a Provider or providers who dispense earthly fortune as well as spiritual health; the demonstration of one's smallness and dependence through the medium of reduced posture and humble gesture; the admission in prayer and song of misdeeds, of misthoughts, and of evil intentions; the admission of inner division and the consequent appeal for inner unification by divine guidance; the need for clearer self-delineation and self-restriction; and finally, the insight that individual trust must become a common faith, individual mistrust a commonly formulated evil, while the individual's need for restoration must become part of the ritual practice of many, and must become a sign of trustworthiness in the community.

Whosoever says he has religion must derive a faith from it which is transmitted to infants in the form of basic trust; whosoever claims that he does not need religion must derive such basic faith from elsewhere.

AUTONOMY VERSUS SHAME AND DOUBT

1

A survey of some of the items discussed in Spock's book under the headings "The One-Year-Old" and "Managing Young Children" will enable those of us who, at this time, do not have such inquisitive creatures in our homes to remember our skirmishes, our victories, and our defeats:

Feeling his oats.
The passion to explore.
He gets more dependent and more independent at the same
    time.

Arranging the house for a wandering baby.
Avoiding accidents.
Now's the time to put poisons out of reach.
How do you make him leave certain things alone?
Dropping and throwing things.
Children learn to control their own aggressive feelings.
Biting humans.
Keeping bedtime happy.
The small child who won't stay in bed at night.

My selection is intended to convey the inventory and range of problems described though I cannot review here either the doctor's excellent advice or his good balance in depicting the remarkable ease and matter-of-factness with which the nursery may be governed at this as at any other stage. Nevertheless, there is an indication of the sinister forces which are leashed and unleashed, especially in the guerilla warfare of unequal wills; for often the child is unequal to his own violent drives, and parent and child are unequal to each other.

The over-all significance of this stage lies in the maturation of the muscle system, the consequent ability (and doubly felt inability) to coordinate a number of highly conflicting action patterns such as "holding on" and "letting go," and the enormous value with which the still highly dependent child begins to endow his autonomous will.

Psychoanalysis has enriched our vocabulary with the word "anality" to designate the particular pleasurableness and willfulness which often attach to the eliminative organs at this stage. The whole procedure of evacuating the bowels and the bladder as completely as possible is, of course, enhanced from the beginning by a premium of "feeling good" which says in effect, "well done." This premium, at the beginning of life, must make up for quite frequent discomfort and tension suffered as the bowels learn to do their daily work. Two developments gradually give these anal experiences the necessary volume: the arrival of better formed stool and the general coordination of the muscle system which permits the development of voluntary release, of dropping and throwing away. This new dimension of approach to things, however, is not restricted to the sphincters. A general ability, indeed, a violent need develops to drop and to throw away and to alternate withholding and expelling at will.

As far as anality proper is concerned, at this point everything depends on whether the cultural environment wants to make something of it. There are cultures where the parents ignore anal behavior and leave it to older children to lead the toddler out to the bushes so that his compliance in this matter may coincide with his wish to imitate the bigger ones. Our Western civilization, and especially certain classes within it, have chosen to take the matter more seriously. It is here that the machine age has added the ideal of a mechanically trained, faultlessly functioning, and always clean, punctual, and deodorized body. In addition it has been more or less consciously assumed that early and rigorous training is absolutely necessary for the kind of personality which will function efficiently in a mechanized world which says "time is money" and which calls for orderliness, punctuality, and thrift. Indications are that in this, we have gone too far; that we have assumed that a child is an animal which must be broken or a machine which must be set and tuned—while, in fact, human virtues can grow only by steps. At any rate our clinical work suggests that the neurotics of our time include the "overcompulsive" type, who is stingy, retentive, and meticulous in matters of affection, time, and money, as well as in matters concerning his bowels. Also, bowel and bladder training has become the most obviously disturbing item of child training in wide circles of our society.

What, then, makes the anal problem potentially important and difficult?

The anal zone lends itself more than any other to the expression of stubborn insistence on conflicting impulses because, for one thing, it is the model zone for two contradictory modes which must become alternating, namely, *retention* and *elimination*. Furthermore, the sphincters are only part of the muscle system with its general ambiguity of rigidity and relaxation, of flexion and extension. This whole stage, then, becomes a battle for *autonomy*. For as he gets ready to stand on his feet more firmly, the infant delineates his world as "I" and "you," "me" and "mine." Every mother knows how astonishingly pliable a child may be at this stage, if and when he has made the decision that he *wants* to do what he is supposed to do. It is impossible, however, to find a reliable formula for making him want to do just that. Every mother knows how lovingly a child at this stage will snuggle and how ruthlessly he will suddenly try to push the adult away. At the same time the child is apt both to hoard things and to discard them, to cling to possessions and to throw them out of the windows of houses and vehicles. All of these seemingly contradictory tendencies, then, we include under the formula of the retentive-eliminative modes.

The matter of mutual regulation between adult and child now faces its severest test. If outer control by too rigid or too early training insists on robbing the child of his attempt *gradually* to control his bowels and other functions willingly and by his free choice, he will again be faced with a double rebellion and a double defeat. Powerless in his own body (sometimes afraid of his bowels) and powerless outside, he will again be forced to seek satisfaction and control either by regression or by fake progression. In other words, he will return to an earlier, oral control, that is, by sucking his thumb and becoming whiny and demanding; or he will become hostile and willful, often using his feces (and, later, dirty words) as ammunition; or he will pretend an autonomy and an ability to do without anybody to lean on which he has by no means really gained.

This stage, therefore, can be decisive for the ratio between love and hate, for that between cooperation and willfulness, and for that between the freedom of self-expression and its suppression. From a sense of *self-control without loss of self-esteem* comes a lasting sense of autonomy and pride; from a sense of muscular and anal impotence, of loss of self-control, and of parental overcontrol comes a lasting sense of doubt and shame.

To develop autonomy, a firmly developed and a convincingly continued stage of early trust is necessary. The infant must come to feel that basic faith in himself and in the world (which is the lasting treasure saved from the conflicts of the oral stage) will not be jeopardized by this sudden violent wish to have a choice, to appropriate demandingly, and to eliminate stubbornly. *Firmness* must protect him against the potential anarchy of his as yet untrained sense of discrimination, his inability to hold on and to let go with circumspection. Yet his environment must back him up in his wish to "stand on his own feet" lest he be overcome by that sense of having exposed himself prematurely and foolishly which we call shame, or that secondary mistrust, that "double take," which we call doubt.

Shame is an infantile emotion insufficiently studied. Shame supposes that one is completely exposed and conscious of being looked at—in a word, self-conscious. One is visible and not ready to be visible; that is why we dream of shame as a situation in which we are stared at in a condition of incomplete dress, in night attire, "with one's pants down." Shame is early expressed in an impulse to bury one's face, or to sink, right then and there, into the ground. This potentiality is abundantly utilized in the educational method of "shaming" used so exclusively by some primitive peoples, where it supplants the often more destructive sense of guilt to be discussed later. The destructiveness of shaming is balanced in some civilizations by devices for "*saving face.*" Shaming exploits an increasing sense of being small, which paradoxically develops as the child stands up and as his awareness permits him to note the relative measures of size and power.

Too much shaming does not result in a sense of propriety but in a secret determination to try to get away with things when unseen, if, indeed, it does not result in deliberate *shamelessness*. There is an impressive American ballad in which a murderer to be hanged on the gallows before the eyes of the community, instead of feeling appropriately afraid or ashamed, begins to berate the onlookers, ending every salvo of defiance with the words, "God damn your eyes." Many a small child, when shamed beyond endurance, may be in a mood (although not in possession of either the courage or the words) to express defiance in similar terms. What I mean by this sinister reference is that there is a limit to a child's and an adult's individual endurance in the face of demands which force him to consider himself, his body, his needs, and his wishes as evil and dirty, and to believe in the infallibility of those who pass such judgment. Occasionally he may be apt to turn things around, to become secretly oblivious to the opinion of others, and to consider as evil only the fact that they exist: his chance will come when they are gone, or when he can leave them.

Many a defiant child, many a young criminal, is of such make-up, and deserves at least an investigation into the conditions which caused him to become that way.

To repeat: muscular maturation sets the stage for experimentation with two simultaneous sets of social modalities—*holding on* and *letting go*. As is the case with all of these modalities, their basic conflicts can lead in the end either to hostile or to benign expectations and attitudes. Thus, "to hold" can become a destructive and cruel retaining or restraining, and it can become a pattern of care: "to have and to hold." To "let go," too, can turn into an inimical letting loose of destructive forces, or it can become a relaxed "to let pass" and "to let be." Culturally speaking, these modalities are neither good nor bad; their value depends on whether their hostile implications are turned against enemy or fellow man—or against the self.

The last-named danger is the one best known to psychiatry. Denied the gradual and well-guided experience of the autonomy of free choice, or weakened by an initial loss of trust, the sensitive child may turn against himself all his urge to discriminate and to manipulate. He will *overmanipulate himself,* he will develop a *precocious conscience.* Instead of taking possession of things in order to test them by repetitive play, he will become obsessed by his own repetitiveness; he will want to have everything "just so," and only in a given sequence and tempo. By such infantile obsessiveness, by dawdling, for example, or by becoming a stickler for certain rituals, the child then learns to gain power over his parents and nurses in areas where he could not find large-scale mutual regulation with them. Such hollow victory, then, is the infantile model for a compulsion neurosis. As for the consequences of this for adult character, they can be observed in the classical compulsive character which we have mentioned. We must add to this the character dominated by the wish to "get away with" things—yet unable to get away even with the wish. For while he learns evasion from others, his precocious conscience does not let him really get away with anything, and he goes through life habitually ashamed, apologetic, and afraid to be seen; or else, in a manner which we call "overcompensatory," he evinces a defiant kind of autonomy. Real inner autonomy, however, is not carried on the sleeve.

2

But it is time to return from these considerations of the abnormal to a study of the headings which transmit the practical and benevolent advice of the children's doctor. They all add up to this: be firm and tolerant with the child at this stage, and he will be firm and tolerant with himself. He will feel pride in being an autonomous person; he will grant autonomy to others; and now and again he will even let himself get away with something.

Why, then, if we know how, do we not tell parents in detail what to do to develop this intrinsic, this genuine autonomy? The answer is: because when it comes to human values, nobody knows how to fabricate or manage the fabrication of the genuine article. My own field, psychoanalysis, having studied particularly the excessive increase of guilt feelings beyond any normal rhyme or reason, and the consequent excessive estrangement of the child from his own body, attempted at least to formulate what should *not* be done to children. These formulations, however, often aroused superstitious inhibitions in those who were inclined to make anxious rules out of vague warnings. Actually, we are learning only gradually what exactly *not* to do with *what kind* of child at *what age*.

People all over the world seem convinced that to make the right (meaning *their)* kind of human being, one must consistently introduce the senses of shame, doubt, guilt, and fear into a child's life. Only the patterns vary. Some cultures begin to restrict early in life, some late, some abruptly, others more gradually. Until enough comparative observations are available, we are apt to add further superstitions, merely because of our wish to *avoid* certain pathological conditions, without even knowing definitely all the factors which are responsible for these conditions. So we say: Don't wean too early; don't train too early. But what is too early and what is too late seem to depend not only on the pathologies we wish to avoid but also on the values we wish to create, or, to put it more honestly, on the values we wish to live by. For no matter what we do in detail, the child will feel primarily what we live by, what makes us loving, cooperative, and firm beings, and what makes us hateful, anxious, and divided in ourselves.

There are of course a few matters of necessary avoidance which become clear from our basic epigenetic point of view. It will be remembered that every new development carries with it its own specific vulnerability. For example, at around eight months the child seems to be somehow more aware, as it were, of his *separateness:* this prepares him for the impending sense of autonomy. At the same time he becomes more cognizant of his mother's features and presence and of the strangeness of others. Sudden or prolonged separation from his mother at that time apparently can cause a sensitive child to experience an aggravation of the experience of division and abandonment, arousing violent anxiety and withdrawal. Again, in the first quarter of the second year, if everything has gone well, the infant just begins to become aware of the autonomy discussed in this chapter. The introduction of bowel training at this time may cause him to resist with all his strength and determination, because he seems to feel that his budding will is being "broken." To avoid this feeling is certainly more important than to insist on his being trained just then because there is a time for the stubborn ascendancy of autonomy and there is a time for the partial sacrifice of secure autonomy, but obviously the time for a meaningful sacrifice is *after* one has acquired and reinforced a core of autonomy and has also acquired more insight.

The more exact localization in time of the most critical growth periods of the personality is becoming established only now. Often, the unavoidable cause of trouble is not one event but the coincidence in time of a number of changes which upset the child's orientation. He may have been involved in a special growth period when the family moved to a new place. Perhaps he was forced to conceive of his first words all over again when the grandmother who had taught him these words suddenly died. A trip on the part of the mother may have exhausted her because she happened to be pregnant at the time, and thus unable, on returning, to make proper amends. Given the right spirit toward life and its vicissitudes, a parent can usually handle such matters, if necessary with the help of the pediatrician or guidance expert. The expert's job, however, should be (to quote Frank Fremont-Smith) *"to set the frame of reference within which choice is permissible and desirable."* For in the last analysis (as comparative studies in child training have convinced many of us) the kind and degree of a sense of autonomy which parents are able to grant their small children depends on the dignity and the sense of personal independence which they derive from their own lives. Again, just as the sense of trust is a reflection of the parents' sturdy and realistic faith, so is the sense of autonomy a reflection of the parents' dignity as individuals.

As was the case with "oral" personality, the compulsive personality (often referred to as "anal" in the psychiatric literature) has its normal aspects and its abnormal exaggerations. If well integrated with other compensatory traits, some compulsiveness is useful in the administration of matters in which order, punctuality, and cleanliness are essential. The question is always whether we remain the masters of the rules by which we want to make things more manageable (not more complicated) or whether the rules master the ruler. But it often happens, in the individual as well as in group life, that the letter of the rules kills the spirit which created them.

3

We have related basic trust to the institution of religion. The basic need of the individual for a delineation of his *autonomy* in the adult order of things seems, in turn, to be taken care of by the *principle of "law and order,"* which in daily life as well as in the high courts of law apportions to each his privileges and his limitations, his obligations and his rights. The sense of autonomy which arises, or should arise, in the second stage of childhood, is fostered by a handling of the small individual which expresses a sense of rightful dignity and lawful independence on the part of the parents and which gives him the confident expectation that the kind of autonomy fostered in childhood will not be frustrated later. This, in turn, necessitates a relationship of parent to parent, of parent to employer, and of parent to government which reaffirms the parent's essential dignity within the hierarchy of social positions. It is important to dwell on this point because much of the shame and doubt, much of the indignity and uncertainty which is aroused in children is a consequence of the parents' frustrations in marriage, in work, and in citizenship. Thus, the sense of autonomy in the child (a sense richly fostered in American childhood in general) must be backed up by the preservation in economic and political life of a high sense of autonomy and of self-reliance.

Social organization assigns with the power of government certain privileges of leadership and certain obligations of conduct; while it imposes on the ruled certain obligations of compliance and certain privileges of remaining autonomous and self-determining. Where this whole matter becomes blurred, however, the matter of individual autonomy becomes an issue of mental health, as well as one of economic reorientation. Where large numbers of people have been prepared in childhood to expect from life a high degree of personal autonomy, pride, and opportunity, and then in later life find themselves ruled by superhuman organizations and machinery too intricate to understand, the result may be deep chronic disappointment not conducive to healthy personalities willing to grant each other a measure of autonomy. All great nations (and all the small ones) are increasingly challenged by the complication and mechanization of modern life, and are being enveloped in the problems of the organization of larger units, larger spheres, and larger interdependencies which by necessity redefine the role of the individual. It is important for the spirit of this country as it is for that of the world, that an increased consciousness of equality and individuality may grow out of the necessity for divided function within the increasing complexity of organization; for otherwise a number of fears are aroused which find expression in anxiety on a large scale, often individually slight and hardly conscious, but nevertheless strangely upsetting to people who seemingly, on the surface, have what they want or what they seem to have a right to expect. Besides irrational fears of losing one's autonomy—"don't fence me in"—there are fears of being sabotaged in one's free will by inner enemies; of being restricted and constricted in one's autonomous initiative; and, paradoxically enough, at the same time of not being completely controlled enough, of not being told what to do. While many such fears are, of course, based on the realistic appraisal of dangers inherent in complex social organizations and in the struggle for power, safety, and security, they seem to contribute to psychoneurotic and psychosomatic disturbances on the one hand, and, on the other, to the easy acceptance of slogans which seem to promise alleviation of conditions by excessive and irrational conformity.

INITIATIVE VERSUS GUILT

1

Having found a firm solution of his problem of autonomy, the child of four and five is faced with the next step—and with the next crisis. Being firmly convinced that he *is* a person, the child must now find out *what kind* of a person he is going to be. And here he hitches his wagon to nothing less than a star: he wants to be like his parents, who to him appear very powerful and very beautiful, although quite unreasonably dangerous. He "identifies with them," he plays with the idea of how it would be to be them. Three strong developments help at this stage, yet also serve to bring the child closer to his crisis: (1) he learns to *move around* more freely and more violently and therefore establishes a wider and, so it seems to him, an unlimited radius of goals; (2) his sense of *language* becomes perfected to the point where he understands and can ask about many things just enough to misunderstand them thoroughly; and (3) both language and locomotion permit him to expand his *imagination* over so many things that he cannot avoid frightening himself with what he himself has dreamed and thought up. Nevertheless, out of all this he must emerge with a sense of *unbroken initiative* as a basis for a high and yet realistic sense of ambition and independence.

One may ask here—one may, indeed—what are the criteria for such an unbroken sense of initiative? The criteria for all the senses discussed here are the same: a crisis, beset with fears, or at least a general anxiousness or tension, seems to be resolved, in that the child suddenly seems to "grow together" both psychologically and physically. He seems to be "more himself," more loving and relaxed and brighter in his judgment (such as it is at this stage). Most of all, he seems to be, as it were, self-activated; he is in the free possession of a certain surplus of energy which permits him to forget failures quickly and to approach what seems desirable (even if it also seems dangerous) with undiminished and better aimed effort. In this way the child and his parents face the next crisis much better prepared.

We are now approaching the end of the third year, when walking is getting to be a thing of ease, or vigor. The books tell us that a child "can walk" much before this; but from the point of view of personality development he cannot really walk as long as he is only able to accomplish the feat more or less well, with more or fewer props, for short spans of time. He has made walking and running an item in his sphere of mastery when gravity is felt to be *within*, when he can forget that he is doing the walking and instead can find out what he can do *with it*. Only then do his legs become an unconscious part of him instead of being an external and still unreliable ambulatory appendix. Only then will he find out with advantage what he now *may* do, along with what he *can* do.

To look back: the first way-station was prone relaxation. The trust based on the experience that the basic mechanisms of breathing, digesting, sleeping, and so forth have a consistent and familiar relation to the foods and comforts offered gives zest to the developing ability to raise oneself to a sitting and then to a standing position. The second way-station (accomplished only toward the end of the second year) is that of being able to sit not only securely but, as it were, untiringly, a feat which permits the muscle system gradually to be used for finer discrimination and for more autonomous ways of selecting and discarding, of piling things up—and of throwing them away with a bang.

The third way-station finds the child able to move independently and vigorously. He is ready to visualize himself as being as big as the perambulating grownups. He begins to make comparisons and is apt to develop untiring curiosity about differences in sizes in general, and sexual differences in particular. He tries to comprehend possible future roles, or at any rate to understand what roles are worth imitating. More immediately, he can now associate with those of his own age. Under the guidance of older children or special women guardians, he gradually enters into the infantile politics of nursery school, street corner, and barnyard. His learning now is eminently intrusive and vigorous: it leads away from his own limitations and into future possibilities.

The *intrusive mode*, dominating much of the behavior of this stage, characterizes a variety of configurationally "similar" activities and fantasies. These include the intrusion into other bodies by physical attack; the intrusion into other people's ears and minds by aggressive talking; the intrusion into space by vigorous locomotion; the intrusion into the unknown by consuming curiosity. The *inclusive mode*, too, can be seen to be generalized in both sexes in experiences of receptivity and tender identification.

This is also the stage of infantile sexual curiosity, genital excitability, and occasional preoccupation and overconcern with sexual matters. This "genitality" is, of course, rudimentary, a mere promise of things to come; often it is not particularly noticeable as such. If not specifically provoked into precocious manifestation by especially strict and pointed prohibitions ("if you touch it, the doctor will cut it off") or special customs (such as sex play in groups), it is apt to lead to no more than a series of fascinating experiences which soon become frightening and pointless enough to be repressed. This leads to the ascendancy of that human specialty which Freud called the "latency" period, that is, the long delay separating infantile sexuality (which in animals is followed by maturity) and physical sexual maturation.

The sexual orientation of the boy is focused on the phallus and its sensations, purposes, and meanings. While erections undoubtedly occur earlier (either reflexively or in response to things and people who make the child feel intensively), a focused interest may now develop in the genitalia of both sexes, as well as an urge to perform playful sex acts, or at least acts of sexual investigation. The increased locomotor mastery and the pride in being big now and *almost* as good as father and mother receives its severest setback in the clear fact that in the genital sphere one is vastly inferior; furthermore, it receives an additional setback in the fact that not even in the distant future is one ever going to be father in sexual relationship to mother, or mother in sexual relationship to father. The very deep emotional consequences of this insight and the magic fears associated with it make up what Freud has called the oedipus complex.

Psychoanalysis verifies the simple conclusion that boys attach their first genital affection to the maternal adults who have otherwise given comfort to their bodies and that they develop their first sexual rivalry against the persons who are the sexual owners of those maternal persons. The little girl, in turn, becomes attached to her father and other important men and jealous of her mother, a development which may cause her much anxiety, for it seems to block her retreat to that selfsame mother, while it makes the mother's disapproval ever so much more magically dangerous because unconsciously "deserved."

Girls often have a difficult time at this stage, because they observe sooner or later that, although their locomotor, mental, and social intrusiveness is increased equally with, and is as adequate as, that of the boys, thus permitting them to become perfect tomboys, they lack one item: the penis; and with it, important prerogatives in some cultures and classes. While the boy has this visible, erectable, and comprehensible organ to which he can attach dreams of adult bigness, the girl's clitoris only poorly sustains dreams of sexual equality. She does not even have breasts as analogously tangible tokens of her future; her maternal drives are relegated to play fantasy or baby tending. On the other hand, where the mother dominates the household, the boy, in turn, can develop a sense of inadequacy because he learns at this stage that while a boy can do well in play and work, he will never boss the house, the mother, and the older sisters. His mother and sisters, in fact, might get even with him for vast doubts in themselves by making him feel that a boy (with his snails and puppy-dog tails) is really an inferior if not a repulsive creature. Both the girl and the boy are now extraordinarily appreciative of any convincing promise of the fact that someday they will be as good as father or mother—perhaps better; and they are grateful for sexual enlightenment, a little at a time, and patiently repeated at intervals. Where the necessities of economic life and the simplicity of its social plan make the male and female roles and their specific powers and rewards comprehensible, the early misgivings about sexual differences are, of course, more easily integrated in the culture's design for the differentiation of sexual roles.

This stage adds to the inventory of basic social modalities in both sexes that of "making" in the older and today slangier sense of "being on the make." There is no simpler, stronger word to match the social modalities previously enumerated. The word suggests enjoyment of competition, insistence on goal, pleasure of conquest. In the boy the emphasis remains on "making" by head-on attack; in the girl it may change to "making" by making herself attractive and endearing. The child thus develops the prerequisites for *masculine* and *feminine initiative*, that is, for the selection of social goals and perserverance in approaching them. Thus the stage is all set for entrance into life, except that life must first be school life. The child here must repress or forget many of the fondest hopes and most energetic wishes, while his exuberant imagination is tamed and he learns the necessary self-restraint and the necessary interest in impersonal things—even the three R's. This often demands a change of personality that is sometimes too drastic for the good of the child. This change is not only a result of education but also of an inner reorientation, and it is based on a biological fact (the delay of sexual maturation) and a psychological one (the repression of childhood wishes). For those sinister oedipal wishes, in consequence of vastly increased imagination and, as it were, the intoxication of increased locomotor powers, are apt to lead to secret fantasies of terrifying proportions. The consequence is a deep sense of *guilt*—a strange sense, for it forever seems to imply that the individual has committed crimes and deeds which, after all, were not only not committed but also would have been biologically quite impossible.

While the struggle for autonomy at its worst concentrated on keeping rivals out, and was therefore more an expression of *jealous rage* most often directed against encroachments by *younger* siblings, initiative brings with it *anticipatory rivalry* with those who were there first and who may therefore occupy with their superior equipment the field toward which one's initiative is directed. Jealousy and rivalry, those often embittered and yet essentially futile attempts at demarcating a sphere of unquestioned privilege, now come to a climax in a final contest for a favored position with one of the parents; the inevitable and necessary failure leads to guilt and anxiety. The child indulges in fantasies of being a giant and a tiger, but in his dreams he runs in terror for dear life. This, then, is the stage of fear for life and limb, including the fear of losing (or on the part of the girl the conviction that she may have lost) the male genital as punishment for the fantasies attached to infantile genital excitement.

All of this may seem strange to readers who have only seen the sunnier side of childhood and have not recognized the potential powerhouse of destructive drives which can be aroused and temporarily buried at this stage, only to contribute later to the inner arsenal of a destructiveness so ready to be used when opportunity provokes it. By using the words "potential," "provoke," and "opportunity," I mean to emphasize that there is little in these inner developments which cannot be harnessed to constructive and peaceful initiative if only we learn to understand the conflicts and anxieties of childhood and the importance of childhood for mankind. But if we should choose to overlook or belittle the phenomena of childhood, or to regard them as "cute" (even as the individual forgets the best and the worst dreams of his childhood), we shall forever overlook one of the eternal sources of human vitality as well as anxiety and strife.

2

It is at this stage of initiative that the great governor of initiative, namely, *conscience*, becomes firmly established. Only as a dependent does man develop conscience, that dependence on himself which makes him, in turn, dependable; and only when thoroughly dependable with regard to a number of fundamental values can he become independent and teach and develop tradition.

The child now feels not only ashamed when found out but also afraid of being found out. He now hears, as it were, God's voice without seeing God. Moreover, he begins automatically to feel guilty even for mere thoughts and for deeds which nobody has watched. This is the cornerstone of morality in the individual sense. But from the point of view of mental health, we must point out that if this great achievement is overburdened by all too eager adults, it can be bad for the spirit and for morality itself. For the conscience of the child *can* be primitive, cruel, and uncompromising, as may be observed in instances where children learn to constrict themselves to the point of over-all inhibition; where they develop an obedience more literal than the one the parent wishes to exact; or where they develop deep regressions and lasting resentments because the parents themselves do not seem to live up to the new conscience which they have fostered in the child. One of the deepest conflicts in life is the hate for a parent who served as the model and the executor of the conscience but who (in some form) was found trying to "get away with" the very transgressions which the child can no longer tolerate in himself. These transgressions often are the natural outcome of the existing inequality between parent and child. Often, however, they represent a thoughtless exploitation of such inequality, with the result that the child comes to feel that the whole matter is not one of universal goodness but of arbitrary power. The suspiciousness and evasiveness which is thus mixed in with the all-or-nothing quality of the superego, that organ of tradition, makes moralistic man a great potential danger to himself and to his fellow men. It is as if morality, to him, became synonymous with vindictiveness and with the suppression of others.

It is necessary to point to the source of such moralism (not to be mistaken for morality) in the child of this age because infantile moralism is a stage to be lived through and worked through. The consequences of the guilt aroused at this stage (guilt expressed in a deep-seated conviction that the child as such, or drive as such, is essentially bad) often do not show until much later, when conflicts over initiative may find expression in a self-restriction which keeps an individual from living up to his inner capacities or to the powers of his imagination and feeling (if not in relative sexual impotence or frigidity). All of this, of course, may in turn be "overcompensated" in a great show of tireless initiative, in a quality of "go-at-itiveness" at all cost. Many adults feel that their worth as people consists entirely in *what they are doing*, or rather in *what they are going to do next*, and not in what they are, as individuals. The strain consequently developed in their bodies, which are always "on the go," with the engine racing, even at moments of rest, is a powerful contribution to the much-discussed psychosomatic diseases of our time.

Pathology, however, is only the sign that valuable human resources are being neglected, that they have been neglected first of all in childhood. The problem is again one of mutual regulation. Where the child, now so ready to overrestrict himself, can gradually develop a sense of responsibility, where he can gain some simple feeling for the institutions, functions, and roles which will permit him to anticipate his responsible participation as an adult, he will soon find pleasurable accomplishment in wielding miniature tools and weapons, in manipulating meaningful toys, and in taking care of himself—and of younger children.

For such is the wisdom of the ground plan that at no time is the individual more ready to learn quickly and avidly, to become big in the sense of sharing obligation, discipline, and performance rather than power, in the sense of *making things, instead of "making" people*, than during this period of his development. He is also eager and able to *make things together*, to combine with other children for the purpose of constructing and planning, instead of trying to boss and coerce them; and he is able and willing to profit fully by the association with teachers and ideal prototypes.

Parents often do not realize why some children suddenly seem to think less of them and seem to attach themselves to teachers, to the parents of other children, or to people representing occupations which the child can grasp: firemen and policemen, gardeners and plumbers. The point is that children do not wish to be reminded of the principal inequality with the parent of the same sex. They remain identified with this same parent; but for the present they look for opportunities where transitory identification seems to promise a field of initiative without too much conflict or guilt.

Often, however (and this seems more typical of the American home than of any other in the world), the child can be guided by the parent himself into a second, a more realistic identification based on the spirit of equality experienced in doing things together. In connection with comprehensible technical tasks, a companionship may develop between father and son, an experience of essential *equality in worth*, in spite of the *inequality in time schedules*. Such companionship is a lasting treasure not only for parent and child but for mankind, which so sorely needs an alleviation of all those hidden hatreds which stem from the exploitation of weakness because of mere size or schedule.

Only a combination of early prevention and alleviation of hatred and guilt in the growing being, and the consequent handling of hatred in the free collaboration of people who feel *equal in worth although different in kind or function or age*, permits a peaceful cultivation of initiative, a truly free sense of enterprise. And the word "enterprise" was deliberately chosen. For a comparative view of child training suggests that it is the prevalent economic ideal, or some of its modifications, which is transmitted to the child at the time when, in identification with his parent, he applies

the dreams of early childhood to the as yet dim goals of an active
adult life.

1

One might say that personality at the first stage crystallizes
around the conviction "I am what I am given," and that of the
second, "I am what I will." The third can be characterized by "I
am what I can imagine I will be." We must now approach the
fourth: "I am what I learn." The child now wants to be shown
how to get busy with something and how to be busy with others.

This trend, too, starts much earlier, especially in some children. They want to watch how things are done and to try doing
them. If they are lucky they live near barnyards or on streets
around busy people and around many other children of all ages, so
that they can watch and try, observe and participate as their
capacities and their initiative grow in tentative spurts. But now it
is time to *go to school*. In all cultures, at this stage, children receive
some systematic instruction, although it is by no means always in
the kind of school which literate people must organize around
teachers who have learned how to teach literacy. In preliterate
people much is learned from adults who become teachers by
acclamation rather than by appointment; and very much is
learned from older children. What is learned in more primitive
surroundings is related to the basic skills of *technology* which are
developed as the child gets ready to handle the utensils, the tools,
and the weapons used by the big people: he enters the technology
of his tribe very gradually but also very directly. More literate
people, with more specialized careers, must prepare the child by
teaching him things which first of all make him literate. He is then

given the widest possible basic education for the greatest number of possible careers. The greater the specialization, the more indistinct the goal of initiative becomes; and the more complicated the social reality, the vaguer the father's and mother's role in it. Between childhood and adulthood, then, our children go to school; and school seems to be a world all by itself, with its own goals and limitations, its achievements and disappointments.

Grammar-school education has swung back and forth between the extreme of making early school life an extension of grim adulthood by emphasizing self-restraint and a strict sense of duty in doing what one is *told* to do, and the other extreme of making it an extension of the natural tendency in childhood to find out by playing, to learn what one must do by doing steps which one *likes* to do. Both methods work for some children at times but not for all children at all times. The first trend, if carried to the extreme, exploits a tendency on the part of the preschool and grammar-school child to become entirely dependent on prescribed duties. He thus learns much that it absolutely necessary and he develops an unshakable sense of duty; but he may never unlearn again an unnecessary and costly self-restraint with which he may later make his own life and other people's lives miserable, and in fact spoil his own children's natural desire to learn and to work. The second trend, when carried to an extreme, leads not only to the well-known popular objection that children do not learn anything any more but also to such feelings in children as are expressed in the by now famous remark of a metropolitan child who apprehensively asked one morning: "Teacher, *must* we do today what we *want* to do?" Nothing could better express the fact that children at this age *do* like to be mildly but firmly coerced into the adventure of finding out that one can learn to accomplish things which one would never have thought of by oneself, things which owe their attractiveness to the very fact that they are *not* the product of play and fantasy but the product of reality, practicality, and logic; things which thus provide a token sense of participation in the real world of adults. In discussions of this kind it is common to say that one must steer a middle course between play and work, between childhood and adulthood, between old-fashioned and progressive education. It is always easy (and it seems entirely satisfactory to one's critics) to say that one plans to steer a middle course, but in practice it often leads to a course charted by avoidances rather than by zestful goals. Instead of pursuing, then, a course which merely avoids the extremes of easy play or hard work, it may be worth while to consider what play is and what work is, and then learn to dose and alternate each in such a way that they play into and work toward each other. Let us review briefly what play may mean at various stages of childhood and adulthood.

The adult plays for purposes of recreation. He steps out of his reality into imaginary realities for which he has made up arbitrary but nonetheless binding rules. But an adult rarely gets away with being a playboy. Only he who works shall play—if, indeed, he can relax his competitiveness.

The playing child, then, poses a problem: whoever does not work shall not play. Therefore, to be tolerant of the child's play the adult must invent theories which show either that childhood play is really the child's work or that it does not count. The most popular theory, and the easiest on the observer, is that the child is nobody yet and that the nonsense of his play reflects it. According to Spencer, play uses up surplus energy in the young of a number of mammalians who do not need to feed or protect themselves because their parents do it for them. Others say that play is either preparation for the future or a method of working off past emotion, a means of finding imaginary relief for past frustrations.

It is true that the content of individual play often proves to be the infantile way of thinking over difficult experiences and of *restoring a sense of mastery*, comparable to the way in which we repeat, in ruminations and in endless talk, in daydreams and in dreams during sleep, experiences that have been too much for us. This is the rationale for play observation, play diagnosis, and play therapy. In watching a child play, the trained observer can get an impression of what it is the child is "thinking over," and what faulty logic, what emotional dead end he may be caught in. As a diagnostic tool such observation has become indispensable.

The small world of manageable toys is a harbor which the child establishes, returning to it when he needs to overhaul his ego. But the thing-world has its own laws: it may resist rearrangement or it may simply break to pieces; it may prove to belong to somebody else and be subject to confiscation by superiors. Thus, play may seduce the child into an unguarded expression of dangerous themes and attitudes which arouse anxiety and lead to sudden *disruption of play*. This is the counterpart, in waking life, of the anxiety dream; it can keep children from trying to play just as the fear of night terror can keep them from going to sleep. If thus frightened or disappointed, the child may regress into daydreaming, thumb sucking, masturbating. On the other hand, if the first use of the thing-world is successful and guided properly, the *pleasure of mastering toy things* becomes associated with the *mastery of the conflicts* which were projected on them and with the *prestige* gained through such mastery.

Finally, at nursery-school age playfulness reaches into the world *shared with others*. At first these others are treated as things; they are inspected, run into, or forced to "be horsie." Learning is necessary in order to discover what potential play content can be admitted only to fantasy or only to play by and with oneself; what content can be successfully represented only in the world of toys and small things; and what content can be shared with others and even forced upon them.

What is infantile play, then? We saw that it is not the equivalent of adult play, that it is not recreation. The playing adult steps sideward into another, an artificial reality; the playing child advances forward to new stages of *real mastery*. This new mastery is not restricted to the technical mastery of toys and *things*; it also includes an infantile way of mastering *experience* by meditating, experimenting, planning, and sharing.

2

While all children at times need to be left alone in solitary play (or later in the company of books and radio, motion pictures and video, all of which, like the fairy tales of old, at least *sometimes* seem to convey what fits the needs of the infantile mind), and while all children need their hours and days of make-believe in games, they all, sooner or later, become dissatisfied and disgruntled without a sense of being useful, without a sense of being able to make things and make them well and even perfectly: this is what I call the *sense of industry*. Without this, the best-entertained child soon acts exploited. It is as if he knows and his society knows that now that he is psychologically already a rudimentary parent, he must begin to be somewhat of a worker and potential provider before becoming a biological parent. With the oncoming latency period, then, the normally advanced child forgets, or rather "sublimates" (that is, applies to more useful pursuits and approved goals) the necessity of "making" people by direct attack or the desire to become father or mother in a hurry: he now learns to win recognition by *producing things*. He develops industry; that is, he adjusts himself to the inorganic laws of the tool world. He can become an eager and abosrbed unit of a productive situation. To bring a productive situation to completion is an aim which gradually supersedes the whims and wishes of his idiosyncratic drives and personal disappointments. As he once untiringly strove to walk well, and to throw things away well, he now wants to make things well. He develops the pleasure of *work completion* by steady attention and persevering diligence.

The danger at this stage is the development of a sense of *inadequacy and inferiority*. This may be caused by an insufficient solution of the preceding conflict: he may still want his mummy more than knowledge; he may still rather be the baby at home than the big child in school; he still compares himself with his father, and the comparison arouses a sense of guilt as well as a sense of anatomical inferiority. Family life (small family) may not have prepared him for school life, or school life may fail to sustain the promises of earlier stages in that nothing that he has learned to do well already seems to count one bit with the teacher. And then, again, he may be potentially able to excel in ways which are dormant and which, if not evoked now, may develop late or never.

Good teachers, healthy teachers, relaxed teachers, teachers who feel trusted and respected by the community, understand all this and can guide it. They know how to alternate play and work, games and study. They know how to recognize special efforts, how to encourage special gifts. They also know how to give a child time, and how to handle those children to whom school, for a while, is not important and rather a matter to endure than to enjoy; or the child to whom, for a while, other children are much more important than the teacher.

Good parents, healthy parents, relaxed parents, feel a need to make their children trust their teachers, and therefore to have teachers who can be trusted. It is not my job here to discuss teacher selection, teacher training, and the status and payment of teachers in their communities—all of which is of direct importance for the development and the maintenance in children of a *sense of industry* and of a positive identification with those who *know* things and know how to *do* things. Again and again I have observed in the lives of especially gifted and inspired people that one teacher, somewhere, was able to kindle the flame of hidden talent.

The fact that the majority of teachers in the elementary schools are women must be considered here in passing, because it often leads to a conflict with the "ordinary" boy's masculine identification, as if knowledge were feminine, action masculine. Both boys and girls are apt to agree with Bernard Shaw's statement that those who can, do, while those who cannot, teach. The selection and training of teachers, then, is vital for the avoidance of the dangers which can befall the individual at this stage. There is, first, the above-mentioned sense of inferiority, the feeling that one will never be any good—a problem which calls for the type of teacher who knows how to emphasize what a child *can* do, and who knows a psychiatric problem when she sees one. Second, there is the danger of the child's identifying too strenuously with a too virtuous teacher or becoming the teacher's pet. What we shall presently refer to as his sense of identity can remain prematurely fixed on being nothing but a good little worker or a good little helper, which may not be all he *could* be. Third, there is the danger (probably the most common one) that throughout the long years of going to school he will never acquire the enjoyment of work and the pride of doing at least one kind of thing well. This is particularly of concern in relation to that part of the nation who do not complete what schooling is at their disposal. It is always easy to say that they are born that way; that there must be less educated people as background for the superior ones; that the market needs and even fosters such people for its many simple and unskilled tasks. But from the point of view of the healthy personality (which, as we proceed, must now include the aspect of playing a constructive role in a healthy society), we must consider those who have had just enough schooling to appreciate what more fortunate people are learning to do but who, for one reason or another, have lacked inner or outer support of their stick-to-itiveness.

It will have been noted that, regarding the period of a developing sense of industry, I have referred to *outer hindrances* but not to any crisis (except a deferred inferiority crisis) coming from the inventory of basic human drives. This stage differs from the others in that it does not consist of a swing from a violent inner upheaval to a new mastery. The reason Freud called it the latency stage is that violent drives are normally dormant at that time. But it is only a lull before the storm of puberty.

On the other hand, this is socially a most decisive stage: since industry involves doing things beside and with others, a first sense of *division of labor* and of *equality of opportunity* develops at this time. When a child begins to feel that it is the color of his skin, the background of his parents, or the cost of his clothes rather than his wish and his will to learn which will decide his social worth, lasting harm may ensue for the *sense of identity*, to which we must now turn.

IDENTITY VERSUS IDENTITY DIFFUSION

1

With the establishment of a good relationship to the world of skills and to those who teach and share the new skills, childhood proper comes to an end. Youth begins. But in puberty and adolescence all sameness and continuities relied on earlier are questioned again because of a rapidity of body growth which equals that of early childhood and because of the entirely new addition of physical genital maturity. The growing and developing young people, faced with this physiological revolution within them, are now primarily concerned with attempts at consolidating their social roles. They are sometimes morbidly, often curiously, preoccupied with what they appear to be in the eyes of others as compared with what they feel they are, and with the question of how to connect the earlier cultivated roles and skills with the ideal prototypes of the day. In their search for a new sense of continuity and sameness, some adolescents have to refight many of the crises of earlier years, and they are never ready to install lasting idols and ideals as guardians of a final identity.

The integration now taking place in the form of the ego identity is more than the sum of the childhood identifications. It is the inner capital accrued from all those experiences of each successive stage, when meaningful identification led to a successful alignment of the individual's *basic drives* with his *endowment* and his *opportunities*. In psychoanalysis we ascribe such successful alignments to "ego synthesis"; I have tried to demonstrate that the ego values accrued in childhood culminate in what I have called *a sense of ego identity*. The sense of ego identity, then, is the accrued confidence that one's ability to maintain inner sameness and continuity (one's ego in the psychological sense) is matched by the sameness and continuity of one's meaning for others. Thus, self-esteem, confirmed at the end of each major crisis, grows to be a conviction that one is learning effective steps toward a tangible future, that one is developing a defined personality within a social reality which one understands. The growing child must, at every step, derive a vitalizing sense of reality from the awareness that his individual way of mastering experience is a successful variant of the way other people around him master experience and recognize such mastery.

In this, children cannot be fooled by empty praise and condescending encouragement. They may have to accept artificial bolstering of their self-esteem in lieu of something better, but what I call their accruing ego identity gains real strength only from wholehearted and consistent recognition of real accomplishment, that is, achievement that has meaning in their culture. On the other hand, should a child feel that the environment tries to deprive him too radically of all the forms of expression which permit him to develop and to integrate the next step in his ego identity, he will resist with the astonishing strength encountered in animals who are suddenly forced to defend their lives. Indeed, in the social jungle of human existence, there is no feeling of being alive without a sense of ego identity. To understand this would be to understand the trouble of adolescents better, especially the trouble of all those who cannot just be "nice" boys and girls, but are desperately seeking for a satisfactory sense of belonging, be it in cliques and gangs here in our country or in inspiring mass movements in others.

Ego identity, then, develops out of a gradual integration of all identifications, but here, if anywhere, the whole has a different quality than the sum of its parts. Under favorable circumstances children have the nucleus of a separate identity in early life; often they must defend it against any pressure which would make them overidentify with one of their parents. This is difficult to learn from patients, because the neurotic ego has, by definition, fallen prey to overidentification and to faulty identifications with disturbed parents, a circumstance which isolated the small individual both from his budding identity and from his milieu. But we can study it profitably in the children of minority-group Americans who, having successfully graduated from a marked and well-guided stage of autonomy, enter the most decisive stage of American childhood: that of initiative and industry.

Minority groups of a lesser degree of Americanization (Negroes, Indians, Mexicans, and certain European groups) often are privileged in the enjoyment of a more sensual early childhood. Their crises come when their parents and teachers, losing trust in themselves and using sudden correctives in order to approach the vague but pervasive Anglo-Saxon ideal, create violent discontinuities; or where, indeed, the children themselves learn to disavow their sensual and overprotective mothers as temptations and a hindrance to the formation of a more American personality.

On the whole, it can be said that American schools successfully meet the challenge of training children of play-school age and of the elementary grades in a spirit of self-reliance and enterprise. Children of these ages seem remarkably free of prejudice and apprehension, preoccupied as they still are with growing and learning and with the new pleasures of association outside their families. This, to forestall the sense of individual inferiority, must lead to a hope for "industrial association," for equality with all those who apply themselves wholeheartedly to the same skills and adventures in learning. Many individual successes, on the other hand, only expose the now overly encouraged children of mixed backgrounds and maybe differing endowments to the shock of American adolescence: the standardization of individuality and the intolerance of "differences."

The emerging ego identity, then, bridges the early childhood stages, when the body and the parent images were given their specific meanings, and the later stages, when a variety of social roles becomes available and increasingly coercive. A lasting ego identity cannot begin to exist without the trust of the first oral stage; it cannot be completed without a promise of fulfillment which from the dominant image of adulthood reaches down into the baby's beginnings and which creates at every step an accruing sense of ego strength.

2

The danger of this stage is *identity diffusion;* as Biff puts it in Arthur Miller's *Death of a Salesman*, "I just can't take hold, Mom, I can't take hold of some kind of a life." Where such a dilemma is based on a strong previous doubt of one's ethnic and sexual identity, delinquent and outright psychotic incidents are not uncommon. Youth after youth, bewildered by some assumed role, a role forced on him by the inexorable standardization of American adolescence, runs away in one form or another; leaving schools and jobs, staying out all night, or withdrawing into bizarre and inaccessible moods. Once "delinquent," his greatest need and often his only salvation, is the refusal on the part of older friends, advisers, and judiciary personnel to type him further by pat diagnoses and social judgments which ignore the special dynamic conditions of adolescence. For if diagnosed and treated correctly, seemingly psychotic and criminal incidents do not in adolescence have the same fatal significance which they have at other ages. Yet many a youth, finding that the authorities expect him to be "a bum" or "a queer," or "off the beam," perversely obliges by becoming just that.

In general it is primarily the inability to settle on an occupational identity which disturbs young people. To keep themselves together they temporarily overidentify, to the point of apparent complete loss of identity, with the heroes of cliques and crowds. On the other hand, they become remarkably clannish, intolerant, and cruel in their exclusion of others who are "different," in skin color or cultural background, in tastes and gifts, and often in entirely petty aspects of dress and gesture arbitrarily selected as *the* signs of an in-grouper or out-grouper. It is important to understand (which does not mean condone or participate in) such intolerance as the necessary *defense against a sense of identity confusion*, which is unavoidable at a time of life when the body changes its proportions radically, when genital maturity floods body and imagination with all manner of drives, when intimacy with the other sex approaches and is, on occasion, forced on the youngster, and when life lies before one with a variety of conflicting possibilities and choices. Adolescents help one another temporarily through such discomfort by forming cliques and by stereotyping themselves, their ideals, and their enemies.

It is important to understand this because it makes clear the appeal which simple and cruel totalitarian doctrines have on the minds of the youth of such countries and classes as have lost or are losing their group identities (feudal, agrarian, national, and so forth) in these times of world-wide industrialization, emancipation, and wider intercommunication. The dynamic quality of the tempestuous adolescences lived through in patriarchal and agrarian countries (countries which face the most radical changes in political structure and in economy) explains the fact that their young people find convincing and satisfactory identities in the simple totalitarian doctrines of race, class, or nation. Even though we may be forced to win wars against their leaders, we still are faced with the job of winning the peace with these grim youths by convincingly demonstrating to them (by living it) a democratic identity which can be strong and yet tolerant, judicious and still determined.

But it is increasingly important to understand this also in order to treat the intolerances of our adolescents at home with understanding and guidance rather than with verbal stereotypes or prohibitions. It is difficult to be tolerant if deep down you are not quite sure that you are a man (or a woman), that you will ever grow together again and be attractive, that you will be able to master your drives, that you really know who you are,[5] that you know what you want to be, that you know what you look like to others, and that you will know how to make the right decisions without, once for all, committing yourself to the wrong friend, sexual partner, leader, or career.   .

Democracy in a country like America poses special problems in that it insists on *self-made identities* ready to grasp many chances and ready to adjust to changing necessities of booms and busts, of peace and war, of migration and determined sedentary life. Our democracy, furthermore, must present the adolescent with ideals which can be shared by youths of many backgrounds and which emphasize autonomy in the form of independence and initiative in the form of enterprise. These promises, in turn, are not easy to fulfill in increasingly complex and centralized systems of economic and political organization, systems which, if geared to war, must automatically neglect the "self-made" identities of millions of individuals and put them where they are most needed. This is hard on many young Americans because their whole upbringing, and therefore the development of a healthy personality, depends on a certain degree of *choice*, a certain hope for an individual *chance*, and a certain conviction in freedom of *self-determination*.

We are speaking here not only of high privileges and lofty ideals but also of psychological necessities. Psychologically speaking, a gradually accruing ego identity is the only safeguard against the *anarchy of drives* as well as the *autocracy of conscience*, that is, the cruel overconscientiousness which is the inner residue in the adult of his past inequality in regard to his parent. Any loss of a sense of identity exposes the individual to his own childhood conflicts—as could be observed, for example, in the neuroses of World War II among men and women who could not stand the general dislocation of their careers or a variety of other special pressures of war. Our adversaries, it seems, understand this. Their psychological warfare consists in the determined continuation of general conditions which permit them to indoctrinate mankind within their orbit with the simple and yet for them undoubtedly effective identities of class warfare and nationalism, while they know that the psychology, as well as the economy, of free enterprise and of self-determination is stretched to the breaking point under the conditions of long-drawn-out cold and lukewarm war. It is clear, therefore, that we must bend every effort to present our young men and women with the tangible and trustworthy promise of opportunities for a rededication to the life for which the country's history, as well as their own childhood, has prepared them. Among the tasks of national defense, this one must not be forgotten.

I have referred to the relationship of the problem of trust to matters of adult faith; to that of the problem of autonomy to matters of adult independence in work and citizenship. I have pointed to the connection between a sense of initiative and the kind of enterprise sanctioned in the economic system, and between the sense of industry and a culture's technology. In searching for the social values which guide identity, one confronts the problem of aristocracy, which in its widest possible sense connotes the conviction that the best people rule and that that rule develops the best in people. In order not to become cynically or apathetically lost, young people in search of an identity must somewhere be able to convince themselves that those who succeed thereby shoulder the obligation of being the best; that is, of personifying the nation's ideals. In this country, as in any other, we have those successful types who become the cynical representatives of the "inside track," the "bosses" of impersonal machinery. In a culture once pervaded with the value of the self-made man, a special danger ensues from the idea of a synthetic personality: as if you are what you can appear to be, or as if you are what you can buy. This can be counteracted only by a system of education that transmits values and goals which determinedly aspire beyond mere "functioning" and "making the grade."

THREE STAGES OF ADULTHOOD

Intimacy and Distantiation versus Self-Absorption

When childhood and youth come to an end, life, so the saying goes, begins: by which we mean work or study for a specified career, sociability with the other sex, and in time, marriage and a family of one's own. But it is only after a reasonable sense of identity has been established that real *intimacy* with the other sex (or, for that matter, with any other person or even with oneself) is possible. Sexual intimacy is only part of what I have in mind, for it is obvious that sexual intimacies do not always wait for the ability to develop a true and mutual psychological intimacy with another person. The youth who is not sure of his identity shies away from interpersonal intimacy; but the surer he becomes of himself, the more he seeks it in the form of friendship, combat, leadership, love, and inspiration. There is a kind of adolescent attachment between boy and girl which is often mistaken either for mere sexual attraction or for love. Except where the mores demand heterosexual behavior, such attachment is often devoted to an attempt at arriving at a definition of one's identity by talking things over endlessly, by confessing what one feels like and what the other seems like, and by discussing plans, wishes, and expectations. Where a youth does not accomplish such intimate relation with others—and, I would add, with his own inner resources—in late adolescence or early adulthood, he may either isolate himself and find, at best, highly stereotyped and formal interpersonal relations (formal in the sense of lacking in spontaneity, warmth, and real exchange of fellowship), or he must seek them in repeated attempts and repeated failures. Unfortunately, many young people marry under such circumstances, hoping to find themselves in finding one another; but alas, the early obligation to act in a defined way, as mates and as parents, disturbs them in the completion of this work on themselves. Obviously, a change of mate is rarely the answer, but rather some wisely guided insight into the fact that the condition of a true twoness is that one must first become oneself.

The counterpart of intimacy is *distantiation:* the readiness to repudiate, to isolate, and, if necessary, to destroy those forces and people whose essence seems dangerous to one's own. This more mature and more efficient repudiation (it is utilized and exploited in politics and in war) is an outgrowth of the blinder prejudices which during the struggle for an identity differentiate sharply and cruelly between the familiar and the foreign. At first, intimate, competitive, and combative relations are experienced with and against the selfsame people. Gradually, a polarization occurs along the lines of the competitive encounter, the sexual embrace, and various forms of aggressive involvement.

Freud was once asked what he thought a normal person should be able to do well. The questioner probably expected a complicated, a "deep" answer. But Freud simply said, *"Lieben und arbeiten"* ("to love and to work"). It pays to ponder on this simple formula; it gets deeper as you think about it. For when Freud said "love," he meant the expansiveness of generosity as well as genital love; when he said "love *and* work," he meant a general work productiveness which would not preoccupy the individual to the extent that his right or capacity to be a sexual and a loving being would be lost.

Psychoanalysis has emphasized *genitality* as one of the chief signs of a healthy personality. Genitality is the potential capacity to develop orgastic potency in relation to a loved partner of the opposite sex. Orgastic potency here means not the discharge of sex products in the sense of Kinsey's "outlets" but heterosexual mutuality, with full genital sensitivity and with an over-all discharge of tension from the whole body. This is a rather concrete way of saying something about a process which we really do not understand. But the idea clearly is that the experience of the climactic mutuality of orgasm provides a supreme example of the mutual regulation of complicated patterns and in some way appeases the potential rages caused by the daily evidence of the oppositeness of male and female, of fact and fancy, of love and hate, of work and play. Satisfactory relations make sexuality less obsessive and sadistic control superfluous. But here the prescription of psychiatry faces overwhelming inner prejudices and situational limitations in parts of the population whose sense of identity is based on the complete subordination of sexuality and, indeed, sensuality to a life of toil, duty, and worship. Here only gradual frank discussion can clarify the respective dangers of traditional rigidity and abrupt or merely superficial change.

Generativity versus Stagnation

The problem of genitality is intimately related to the seventh criterion of mental health, which concerns parenthood. Sexual mates who find, or are on the way to finding, true genitality in their relations will soon wish (if, indeed, developments wait for the express wish) to combine their personalities and energies in the production and care of common offspring. The pervasive development underlying this wish I have termed *generativity*, because it concerns the establishment (by way of genitality and genes) of the next generation. No other fashionable term, such as "creativity" or "productivity," seems to me to convey the necessary idea.[6] Generativity is primarily the interest in establishing and guiding the next generation, although there are people who, from misfortune or because of special and genuine gifts in other directions, do not apply this drive to offspring but to other forms of altruistic concern and of creativity, which may absorb their kind of parental responsibility. The principal thing is to realize that this is a stage of the growth of the healthy personality and that where such enrichment fails, together, regression from generativity to an obsessive need for pseudo intimacy takes place, often with a pervading sense of stagnation and interpersonal impoverishment. Individuals who do not develop generativity often begin to indulge themselves as if they were their own one and only child. The mere fact of having or even wanting children does not itself attest to generativity; in fact the majority of young parents seen in child-guidance work suffer, it seems, from the retardation of or inability to develop this stage. The reasons are often to be found in early childhood impressions; in faulty identifications with parents; in excessive self-love based on a too strenuously self-made personality; and finally (and here we return to the beginnings) in the lack of some faith, some "belief in the species," which would make a child appear to be a welcome trust of the community.

Integrity versus Despair and Disgust

Only he who in some way has taken care of things and people and has adapted himself to the triumphs and disappointments of being, by necessity, the originator of others and the generator of things and ideas—only he may gradually grow the fruit of the seven stages. I know no better word for it than *integrity*. Lacking a clear definition, I shall point to a few attributes of this state of mind. It is the acceptance of one's own and only life cycle and of the people who have become significant to it as something that had to be and that, by necessity, permitted of no substitutions. It thus means a new different love of one's parents, free of the wish that they should have been different, and an acceptance of the fact that one's life is one's own responsibility. It is a sense of comradeship with men and women of distant times and of different pursuits, who have created orders and objects and sayings conveying human dignity and love. Although aware of the relativity of all the various life styles which have given meaning to human striving, the possessor of integrity is ready to defend the dignity of his own life style against all physical and economic threats. For he knows that an individual life is the accidental coincidence of but one life cycle with but one segment of history; and that for him all human integrity stands and falls with the one style of integrity of which he partakes.

This, then, is a beginning for a formulation of integrity based on clinical and anthropological experience: it is here, above all else, where each reader and each study group must continue to develop in his or its own terms what I have gropingly begun in mine. But I can add, clinically, that the lack or loss of this accrued ego integration is signified by despair and an often unconscious fear of death: the one and only life cycle is not accepted as the ultimate of life. Despair expresses the feeling that the time is short, too short for the attempt to start another life and to try out alternate roads to integrity. Such a despair is often hidden behind a show of disgust, a misanthropy, or a chronic contemptuous displeasure with particular institutions and particular people—a disgust and a displeasure which (where not allied with constructive ideas and a life of cooperation) only signify the individual's contempt of himself.

Ego integrity, therefore, implies an emotional integration which permits participation by followership as well as acceptance of the responsibility of leadership: both must be learned and practiced in religion and in politics, in the economic order and in technology, in aristocratic living, and in the arts and sciences.

CONCLUSION

At this point, I have come close to overstepping the limits (some will say I have long and repeatedly overstepped them) that separate psychology from ethics. But in suggesting that parents, teachers, and doctors must learn to discuss matters of human relations and of community life if they wish to discuss their children's needs and problems, I am only insisting on a few basic psychological insights, which I shall try to formulate briefly in conclusion.

We have, in the last few decades, learned more about the development and growth of the individual and about his motivations (especially unconscious motivations) than in the whole of human history before us (excepting, of course, the implicit wisdom expressed in the Bible or Shakespeare). Increasing numbers of us come to the conclusion that a child and even a baby—perhaps even the fetus—sensitively reflect the quality of the milieu in which they grow up. Children feel the tensions, insecurities, and rages of their parents even if they do not know their causes or witness their most overt manifestations. Therefore, you cannot fool children. Yet, rapid changes in the milieu often make it hard to know whether one must be genuine *against* a changing milieu or whether one may hope for a chance to do one's bit in the way of bettering or stabilizing conditions. It is difficult, also, because in a changing world we are trying out—we must try out—new ways. To bring up children in personal and tolerant ways, based on information and education as well as on tradition, is a very new way: it exposes parents to many additional insecurities, which are temporarily increased by psychiatry, for psychiatric thinking sees the world so full of dangers that it is hard to relax one's caution. I, too, have pointed to as many dangers as to constructive avenues of action. Perhaps we can hope that this is only an indication that we are progressing through one stage of learning. When a man learns how to drive, he must become conscious of all the things that *might* happen; and he must learn to hear and see and read all the danger signals on his dashboard and along the road. Yet he may hope that some day, when he has outgrown this stage of learning, he will be able to glide with the greatest of ease through the landscape, enjoying the view with the confident knowledge that he will react to signs of mechanical trouble or road obstruction with automatic and effective speed.

We are now working toward, and fighting for, a world in which the harvest of democracy may be reaped. But if we want to make the world safe for democracy, we must first make democracy safe for the healthy child. In order to ban autocracy, exploitation, and inequality in the world, we must first realize that the first inequality in life is that of child and adult. Human childhood is long, so that parents and schools may have time to accept the child's personality in trust and to help it to be disciplined and human in the best sense known to us. This long childhood exposes the child to grave anxieties and to a lasting sense of insecurity which, if unduly and senselessly intensified, persists in the adult in the form of vague anxiety—anxiety which, in turn, contributes specifically to the tension of personal, political and even international life. This long childhood exposes adults to the temptation of thoughtlessly and often cruelly exploiting the child's dependence. We make them pay for psychological debts owed to us by others; we make them the victim of tensions which we will not, or dare not, correct in ourselves or in our surroundings. We have learned not to stunt a child's growing body with child labor; we must now learn not to break his growing spirit by making him the victim of our anxieties.

If we will only learn to let live, the plan for growth is all there.

3

The Problem of
Ego Identity

IN A NUMBER of writings (Erikson, 1946, 1950a, 1950b, 1951a) I have been using the term *ego identity* to denote certain comprehensive gains which the individual, at the end of adolescence, must have derived from all of his preadult experience in order to be ready for the tasks of adulthood. My use of this term reflected the dilemma of a psychoanalyst who was led to a new concept not by theoretical preoccupation but rather through the expansion of his clinical awareness to other fields (social anthropology and comparative education) and through the expectation that such expansion would, in turn, profit clinical work. Recent clinical observations have, I feel, begun to bear out this expectation. I have, therefore, gratefully accepted two opportunities[1] offered me to restate and review the problem of identity. The present paper combines both of these presentations. The question before us is whether the concept of identity is essentially a psychosocial one,

This paper was first published in *The Journal of the American Psychoanalytic Association*, 4:56–121, 1956. The work on which this paper is based is supported by a grant of the Field Foundation to the Riggs Center.

or deserves to be considered as a legitimate part of the psycho-analytic theory of the ego.

First a word about the term "identity." As far as I know Freud used it only once in a more than incidental way, and then with a psychosocial connotation. It was when he tried to formulate his link to the Jewish people that he spoke of an "inner identity"[2] which was less based on race or religion than on a common readiness to live in opposition, and on a common freedom from prejudices which narrow the use of the intellect. Here, the term "identity" points to an individual's link with the unique values, fostered by a unique history, of his people. Yet, it also relates to the cornerstone of this individual's unique development: for the importance of the theme of "incorruptible observation at the price of professional isolation" playing a central role in Freud's life (Erikson, 1954). It is this identity of something in the individual's core with an essential aspect of a group's inner coherence which is under consideration here: for the young individual must learn to be most himself where he means most to others—those others, to be sure, who have come to mean most to him. The term "identity" expresses such a mutual relation in that it connotes both a persistent sameness within oneself (selfsameness) and a persistent sharing of some kind of essential character with others.

I can attempt to make the subject matter of identity more explicit only by approaching it from a variety of angles—biographic, pathographic, and theoretical; and by letting the term "identity" speak for itself in a number of connotations. At one time, then, it will appear to refer to a conscious *sense of individual identity*; at another to an unconscious striving for a *continuity of personal character*; at a third, as a criterion for the silent doings of *ego synthesis*; and, finally, as a maintenance of an inner *solidarity* with a group's ideals and identity. In some respects the term will appear to be colloquial and naïve; in others, vaguely related to existing concepts in psychoanalysis and sociology. If, after an attempt at clarifying this relation, the term itself still retains some ambiguity, it will, so I hope, nevertheless have helped to delineate a significant problem, and a necessary point of view.

I begin with one extreme aspect of the problem as exemplified in the biography of an outstanding individual—an individual who labored as hard on the creation of a world-wide *public identity* for himself as he worked on his literary masterpieces.

BIOGRAPHIC: G. B. S. (70) ON
GEORGE BERNARD SHAW (20)

When George Bernard Shaw was a famous man of seventy, he was called upon to review and to preface the unsuccessful work of his early twenties, namely, the two volumes of fiction which had never been published. As one would expect, Shaw proceeded to make light of the production of his young adulthood, but not without imposing on the reader a detailed analysis of young Shaw. Were Shaw not so deceptively witty in what he says about his younger years, his observations probably would have been recognized as a major psychological achievement. Yet, it is Shaw's mark of identity that he eases and teases his reader along a path of apparent superficialities and sudden depths. I dare to excerpt him here for my purposes only in the hope that I will make the reader curious enough to follow him at every step of his exposition (Shaw, 1952).

G. B. S. (for this is the public identity which was one of his masterpieces) describes young Shaw as an "extremely disagreeable and undesirable" young man, "not at all reticent of diabolical opinion," while inwardly "suffering . . . from simple cowardice . . . and horribly ashamed of it." "The truth is," he concludes, "that all men are in a false position in society until they have realized their possibilities and imposed them on their neighbors. They are tormented by a continual shortcoming in themselves; yet they irritate others by a continual overweening. This discord can be resolved by acknowledged success or failure only: everyone is ill at ease until he has found his natural place, whether it be above or below his birthplace." But Shaw must always exempt himself from any universal law which he inadvertently pronounces; so he adds: "This finding of one's place may be made very puzzling by the fact that there is no place in ordinary society for extraordinary individuals."

Shaw proceeds to describe a crisis (of the kind which we will refer to as an *identity crisis*) at the age of twenty. It is to be noted that this crisis was not caused by lack of success or the absence of a defined role but by too much of both: "I made good in spite of myself, and found, to my dismay, that Business, instead of expelling me as the worthless imposter I was, was fastening upon me with no intention of letting me go. Behold me, therefore, in my twentieth year, with a business training, in an occupation which I detested as cordially as any sane person lets himself detest anything he cannot escape from. In March 1876 I broke loose." Breaking loose meant to leave family and friends, business and Ireland, and to avoid the danger of success without identity, of a success unequal to "the enormity of my unconscious ambition." He granted himself a prolongation of the interval between youth and adulthood, which we will call a *psychosocial moratorium*. He writes: ". . . when I left my native city I left this phase behind me, and associated no more with men of my age until, after about eight years of solitude in this respect, I was drawn into the Socialist revival of the early eighties, among Englishmen intensely serious and burning with indignation at very real and very fundamental evils that affected all the world." In the meantime, he seemed to avoid opportunities, sensing that "behind the conviction that they could lead to nothing that I wanted, lay the unspoken fear that they might lead to something I did not want." This *occupational* part of the moratorium was reinforced by an *intellectual* one: "I cannot learn anything that does not interest me. My memory is not indiscriminate; it rejects and selects; and its selections are not academic. . . . I congratulate myself on this;

for I am firmly persuaded that every unnatural activity of the brain is as mischievous as any unnatural activity of the body. . . . Civilization is always wrecked by giving the governing classes what is called secondary education. . . ."

Shaw settled down to study and to write as he pleased, and it was then that the extraordinary workings of an extraordinary personality came to the fore. He managed to abandon the *kind* of work he had been doing without relinquishing the work *habit*: "My office training had left me with a habit of doing something regularly every day as a fundamental condition of industry as distinguished from idleness. I knew I was making no headway unless I was doing this, and that I should never produce a book in any other fashion. I bought supplies of white paper, demy size, by sixpence-worths at a time; folded it in quarto; and condemned myself to fill five pages of it a day, rain or shine, dull or inspired. I had so much of the schoolboy and the clerk still in me that if my five pages ended in the middle of a sentence I did not finish it until the next day. On the other hand, if I missed a day, I made up for it by doing a double task on the morrow. On this plan I produced five novels in five years. It was my professional apprenticeship. . . ." We may add that these first five novels were not published for over fifty years; but Shaw had learned to write as he worked, and to wait as he wrote. How important such initial *ritualization of his worklife* was for the young man's inner defenses may be seen from one of those casual (in fact, parenthetical) remarks with which the great wit almost coyly admits his psychological insight: "I have risen by sheer gravitation, too industrious by acquired habit to stop working (*I work as my father drank*)."[3] He thus points to that combination of *addictiveness* and *compulsivity* which we see as the basis of much pathology in late adolescence and of some accomplishment in young adulthood.

His father's "drink neurosis" Shaw describes in detail, finding in it one of the sources of his biting humor: "It had to be either a family tragedy or family joke." For his father was not "convivial, nor quarrelsome, nor boastful, but miserable, racked with shame and remorse." However, the father had a "humorous sense of anticlimax which I inherited from him and used with much effect when I became a writer of comedy. His anticlimaxes depended for their effect on our sense of the sacredness (of the subject matter). . . . It seems providential that I was driven to the essentials of religion by the reduction of every factitious or fictitious element in it to the most irreverent absurdity."

A more unconscious level of Shaw's oedipal tragedy is represented—with dreamlike symbolism—in what looks like a screen memory conveying his father's impotence: "A boy who has seen 'the governor' with an *imperfectly wrapped-up goose under one arm* and *a ham in the same condition under the other* (both purchased under heaven knows what delusion of festivity) *butting* at the garden wall in the belief that he was *pushing open the gate*, and *transforming his tall hat to a concertina* in the process, and who, instead of being overwhelmed with shame and anxiety at the spectacle, has been so *disabled by merriment* (uproariously shared by the maternal uncle) that he has hardly been able to rush to the rescue of the hat and pilot its wearer to safety, is clearly not a boy who will make tragedies of trifles instead of *making trifles of tragedies*. If you cannot get rid of the family skeleton, you may as well make it dance." It is obvious that the analysis of the psychosexual elements in Shaw's identity could find a solid anchor point in this memory.

Shaw explains his father's downfall with a brilliant analysis of the socioeconomic circumstances of his day. For the father was "second cousin to a baronet, and my mother the daughter of a country gentleman whose rule was, when in difficulties, mortgage. That was my sort of poverty." His father was "the younger son of a younger son of a younger son" and he was "a downstart and the son of a downstart." Yet, he concludes: "To say that my father could not afford to give me a university education is like saying that he could not afford to drink, or that I could not afford to become an author. Both statements are true; but he drank and I became an author all the same."

His mother he remembers for the "one or two rare and delightful occasions when she buttered my bread for me. She buttered it thickly instead of merely wiping a knife on it." Most of the time, however, he says significantly, she merely "accepted me as a natural and customary phenomenon and took it for granted that I should go on occurring in that way." There must have been something reassuring in this kind of impersonality, for "technically speaking, I should say she was the worst mother conceivable, always, however, within the limits of the fact that she was incapable of unkindness to any child, animal, or flower, or indeed to any person or thing whatsoever. . . ." If this could not be considered either a mother's love or an education, Shaw explains: "I was badly brought up because my mother was so well brought up. . . . In her righteous reaction against . . . the constraints and tyrannies, the scoldings and browbeatings and punishments she had suffered in her childhood . . . she reached a negative attitude in which having no substitute to propose, she carried domestic anarchy as far as in the nature of things it can be carried." All in all, Shaw's mother was "a thoroughly disgusted and disillusioned woman . . . suffering from a hopelessly disappointing husband and three uninteresting children grown too old to be petted like the animals and the birds she was so fond of, to say nothing of the humiliating inadequacy of my father's income."

Shaw had really three parents, the third being a man named Lee ("meteoric," "impetuous," "magnetic"), who gave Shaw's mother lessons in singing, not without revamping the whole Shaw household as well as Bernard's ideals: "Although he supplanted my father as the dominant factor in the household, and appropriated all the activity and interest of my mother, he was so completely absorbed in his musical affairs that there was no friction and hardly any intimate personal contacts between the two men: certainly no unpleasantness. At first his ideas astonished us. He said that people should sleep with their windows open. The daring of this appealed to me; and I have done so ever since. He ate brown bread instead of white: a startling eccentricity."

Of the many elements of identity formations which ensued from such a perplexing picture, let me single out only three, selected, simplified, and named for this occasion by me.

The Snob

"As compared with similar English families, we had a power of derisive dramatization that made the bones of the Shavian skeletons rattle more loudly." Shaw recognizes this as "family snobbery mitigated by the family sense of humor." On the other hand, "though my mother was not consciously a snob, the divinity which hedged an Irish lady of her period was not acceptable to the British suburban parents, all snobs, who were within her reach (as customers for private music lessons)." Shaw had "an enormous contempt for family snobbery," until he found that one of his ancestors was an Earl of Fife: "It was as good as being descended from Shakespeare, whom I had been unconsciously resolved to reincarnate from my cradle."

The Noisemaker

All through his childhood, Shaw seems to have been exposed to an oceanic assault of music making: the family played trombones and ophicleides, violoncellos, harps, and tambourines—and, most of all (or is it worst of all) they sang. Finally, however, he taught himself the piano, and this with dramatic noisiness. "When I look back on all the banging, whistling, roaring, and growling inflicted on nervous neighbors during this process of education, I am consumed with useless remorse. . . . I used to drive [my mother] nearly crazy by my favorite selections from Wagner's Ring, which to her was 'all recitative,' and horribly discordant at that. She never complained at the time, but confessed it after we separated, and said that she had sometimes gone away to cry. If I had committed a murder I do not think it would trouble my conscience very much; but this I cannot bear to think of." That, in fact, he may have learned the piano in order to get even with his musical tormentors, he does not profess to realize. Instead, he compromised by becoming—a music *critic*, i.e., one who *writes* about the noise made by others. As a critic, he chose the *nom de plume* Corno di Bassetto—actually the name of an instrument which nobody knew and which is so meek in tone that "not even the devil could make it sparkle." Yet Bassetto became a sparkling critic, and more: "I cannot deny that Bassetto was occasionally vulgar; but that does not matter if he makes you laugh. Vulgarity is a necessary part of a complete author's equipment; and the clown is sometimes the best part of the circus."

The Diabolical One

How the undoubtedly lonely little boy (whose mother listened only to the musical noisemakers) came to use his imagination to converse with a great imaginary companion is described thus: "In my childhood I exercised my literary genius by composing my own prayers . . . they were a literary performance for the enter-tainment and propitiation of the Almighty." In line with his family's irreverence in matters of religion, Shaw's piety had to find and rely on the rock bottom of religiosity which, in him, early became a mixture of "intellectual integrity . . . synchronized with the dawning of moral passion." At the same time it seems that Shaw was (in some unspecified way) a little devil of a child. At any rate, he did not feel identical with himself when he was good: "Even when I was a good boy, I was so only theatrically, because, as actors say, I saw myself in the character." And indeed, at the completion of his identity struggle, i.e., "when Nature completed my countenance in 1880 or thereabouts (I had only the tenderest sprouting of hair on my face until I was 24), I found myself equipped with the upgrowing moustaches and eyebrows, and the sarcastic nostrils of the operatic fiend whose airs (by Gounod) I had sung as a child, and whose attitudes I had affected in my boyhood. Later on, as the generations moved past me, I . . . began to perceive that imaginative fiction is to life what the sketch is to the picture or the conception to the statue."

Thus G.B.S., more or less explicitly, traces his own roots. Yet, it is well worth noting that what he finally *became* seems to him to have been as *innate* as the intended reincarnation of Shakespeare referred to above. His teacher, he says, "puzzled me with her attempts to teach me to read; for I can remember no time at which a page of print was not intelligible to me, and can only suppose that I was born literate." However, he thought of a number of professional choices: "As an alternative to being a Michelangelo I had dreams of being a Badeali (note, by the way, that of literature I had no dreams at all any more than a duck has of swimming)."

He also calls himself "a born Communist" (which, we hasten to say, means a Fabian Socialist), and he explains the peace that comes with the *acceptance of what one seems to be made to be;* the "born Communist . . . knows where he is, and where this society which has so intimidated him is. He is cured of his MAUVAISE HONTE. . . ." Thus "the complete outsider" gradually became his kind of complete insider: "I was," he said, "outside society, outside politics, outside sport, outside the Church"—but this "only within the limits of British barbarism. . . . The moment music, painting, literature, or science came into question the positions were reversed: it was I who was the Insider."

As he traces all of these traits back into childhood, Shaw becomes aware of the fact that only a *tour de force* could have integrated them all: ". . . if I am to be entirely communicative on this subject, I must add that the mere rawness which so soon rubs off was complicated by a deeper strangeness which has made me all my life a sojourner on this planet rather than a native of it. Whether it be that I was born mad or a little too sane, my kingdom was not of this world: I was at home only in the realm of my imagination, and at my ease only with the mighty dead. Therefore, I had to become an actor, and create for myself a fantastic personality fit and apt for dealing with men, and adaptable to the various parts I had to play as author, journalist, orator, politician, committee man, man of the world, and so forth. In this," so Shaw concludes significantly, "I succeeded later on only too well." This statement is singularly illustrative of that faint disgust with which older men at times review the inextricable identity which they had come by in their youth—a disgust which in the lives of some can become mortal despair and psychosomatic involvement.

The end of his crisis of younger years Shaw sums up in these words: "I had the intellectual habit; and by natural combination of critical faculty with literary resource needed only a clear comprehension of life in the light of an intelligible theory: in short, a religion, to set it in triumphant operation." Here the old Cynic has circumscribed in one sentence what the identity formation of any human being must add up to. To translate this into terms more conducive to discussion in ego-psychological and psychosocial terms: Man, to take his place in society, must acquire a "conflict-free," habitual use of a dominant *faculty*, to be elaborated in an *occupation*; a limitless *resource*, a feedback, as it were, from the immediate *exercise* of this occupation, from the *companionship* it provides, and from its *tradition*; and finally, an intelligible *theory* of the processes of life which the old atheist, eager to shock to the last, calls a religion. The Fabian Socialism to which he, in fact, turned is rather an *ideology*, to which general terms we shall adhere, for reasons which permit elucidation only at the end of this paper.

GENETIC: IDENTIFICATION AND IDENTITY

1

The autobiographies of extraordinary (and extraordinarily self-perceptive) individuals are a suggestive source of insight into the development of identity. In order to find an anchor point for the discussion of the universal genetics of identity, however, it would be well to trace its development through the life histories or through significant life episodes of "ordinary" individuals—individuals whose lives have neither become professional autobiographies (as did Shaw's) nor case histories, such as will be discussed in the next chapter. I will not be able to present such material here; I must, instead, rely on impressions from daily life, from participation in one of the rare "longitudinal" studies of the personality development of children,[4] and from guidance work with mildly disturbed young people.

Adolescence is the last and the concluding stage of childhood. The adolescent process, however, is conclusively complete only when the individual has subordinated his childhood identifications to a new kind of identification, achieved in absorbing sociability and in competitive apprenticeship with and among his age-mates. These new identifications are no longer characterized by the playfulness of childhood and the experimental zest of youth: with dire urgency they force the young individual into choices and decisions which will, with increasing immediacy, lead to a more final self-definition, to irreversible role pattern, and thus to commitments "for life." The task to be performed here by the young person and by his society is formidable; it necessitates, in different individuals and in different societies, great variations in the duration, in the intensity, and in the ritualization of adolescence. Societies offer, as individuals require, more or less sanctioned intermediary periods between childhood and adulthood, institutionalized *psychosocial moratoria*, during which a lasting pattern of "inner identity" is scheduled for relative completion.

In postulating a "latency period" which precedes puberty, psychoanalysis has given recognition to some kind of *psychosexual moratorium* in human development—a period of delay which permits the future mate and parent first to "go to school" (i.e., to undergo whatever schooling is provided for in his technology) and to learn the technical and social rudiments of a work situation. It is not within the confines of the libido theory, however, to give an adequate account of a second period of delay, namely, adolescence. Here the sexually matured individual is more or less retarded in his psychosexual capacity for intimacy and in the psychosocial readiness for parenthood. The period can be viewed as a *psychosocial moratorium* during which the individual through free role experimentation may find a niche in some section of his society, a niche which is firmly defined and yet seems to be uniquely made for him. In finding it the young adult gains an assured sense of inner continuity and social sameness which will bridge what he *was* as a child and what he is *about to become*, and will reconcile his *conception of himself* and his community's recognition of him.

If, in the following, we speak of the community's response to the young individual's need to be "recognized" by those around him, we mean something beyond a mere recognition of achievement; for it is of great relevance to the young individual's identity formation that he be responded to, and be given function and status as a person whose gradual growth and transformation make sense to those who begin to make sense to him. It has not been sufficiently recognized in psychoanalysis that such recognition provides an entirely indispensable support to the ego in the specific tasks of adolescing, which are: to maintain the most important ego defenses against the vastly growing intensity of impulses (now invested in a matured genital apparatus and a powerful muscle system); to learn to consolidate the most important "conflict-free" achievements in line with work opportunities; and to resynthesize all childhood identifications in some unique way, and yet in concordance with the roles offered by some wider section of society—be that section the neighborhood block, an anticipated occupational field, an association of kindred minds, or, perhaps (as in Shaw's case) the "mighty dead."

2

Linguistically as well as psychologically, identity and identification have common roots. Is identity, then, the mere sum of earlier identifications, or is it merely an additional set of identifications?

The limited usefulness of the *mechanism of identification* becomes at once obvious if we consider the fact that none of the identifications of childhood (which in our patients stand out in such morbid elaboration and mutual contradiction) could, if merely added up, result in a functioning personality. True, we usually believe that the task of psychotherapy is the replacement of morbid and excessive identifications by more desirable ones. But as every cure attests, "more desirable" identifications tend to be quietly subordinated to a new, a unique Gestalt which is more than the sum of its parts. The fact is that identification as a mechanism is of limited usefulness. Children, at different stages of their development, identify with those *part aspects* of people by which they themselves are most immediately affected, whether in reality or fantasy. Their identifications with parents, for example, center in certain overvalued and ill-understood body parts, capacities, and role appearances. These part aspects, furthermore, are favored not because of their social acceptability (they often are everything but the parents' most adjusted attributes) but by the nature of infantile fantasy which only gradually gives way to a more realistic anticipation of social reality. The final identity, then, as fixed at the end of adolescence is superordinated to any single identification with individuals of the past: it includes all significant identifications, but it also alters them in order to make a unique and a reasonably coherent whole of them.

If we, roughly speaking, consider introjection-projection, identification, and identity formation to be the steps by which the ego grows in ever more mature interplay with the identities of the child's models, the following psychosocial schedule suggests itself:

The mechanisms of *introjection and projection*, which prepare the basis for later identifications, depend for their relative integration on the satisfactory mutuality (Erikson, 1950a) between the *mothering adult(s) and the mothered child*. Only the experience of such mutuality provides a safe pole of self-feeling from which the child can reach out for the other pole: his first love "objects."

The fate of *childhood identifications*, in turn, depends on the child's satisfactory interaction with a trustworthy and meaningful hierarchy of roles as provided by the generations living together in some form of *family*.

Identity formation begins where the usefulness of multiple identification ends. It arises from the selective repudiation and mutual assimilation of childhood identifications, and their absorption in a new configuration, which in turn, is dependent on the process by which a *society* (often through subsocieties) *identifies the young individual*, recognizing him as somebody who had to become the way he is, and who, being the way he is, is taken for granted. The community, often not without some initial mistrust, gives such recognition with a (more or less institutionalized) display of surprise and pleasure in making the acquaintance of a newly emerging individual. For the community, in turn, feels "recognized" by the individual who cares to ask for recognition; it can, by the same token, feel deeply—and vengefully—rejected by the individual who does not seem to care.

3

While the end of adolescence thus is the stage of an overt identity *crisis*, identity *formation* neither begins nor ends with adolescence: it is a lifelong development largely unconscious to the individual and to his society. Its roots go back all the way to the first self-recognition: in the baby's earliest exchange of smiles there is something of a *self-realization coupled with a mutual recognition*.

All through childhood tentative crystallizations take place which make the individual feel and believe (to begin with the most conscious aspect of the matter) as if he approximately knew who he was—only to find that such self-certainty ever again falls prey to the discontinuities of psychosocial development (Benedict, 1938). An example would be the discontinuity between the demands made in a given milieu on a little boy and those made on a "big boy" who, in turn, may well wonder why he was first made to believe that to be little is admirable, only to be forced to exchange this effortless status for the special obligations of one who is "big now." Such discontinuities can amount to a crisis and demand a decisive and strategic repatterning of action, and with it, *compromise* which can be compensated for only by a consistently accruing sense of the social value of such increasing commitment. The cute or ferocious or good small boy, who becomes a studious or gentlemanly or tough big boy must be able—and must be enabled—to combine both sets of values in a recognized identity which permits him, in work and play, and in official and in intimate behavior, to be (and to let others be) a big boy *and* a little boy.

The community supports such development to the extent to which it permits the child, at each step, to orient himself toward a complete *"life plan"* with a hierarchical order of roles as represented by individuals of different age grades. Family, neighborhood, and school provide contact and experimental identification with younger and older children and with young and old adults. A child, in the multiplicity of successive and tentative identifications, thus begins early to build up expectations of what it will be like to be older and what it will feel like to have been younger—expectations which become part of an identity as they are, step by step, verified in decisive experiences of psychosocial "fittedness."

4

The *critical phases* of life have been described in psychoanalysis primarily in terms of instincts and defenses, i.e., as "typical danger situations" (Hartmann, 1939). Psychoanalysis has concerned itself more with the encroachment of psychosexual crises on psychosocial (and other) functions than with the specific crisis created by the maturation of each function. Take for example a child who is learning to *speak:* he is acquiring one of the prime functions supporting a sense of individual autonomy and one of the prime techniques for expanding the radius of give-and-take. The mere indication of an ability to give intentional sound-signs immediately obligates the child to "*say* what he wants." It may force him to *achieve* by proper verbalization the attention which was afforded him previously in response to mere gestures of needfulness. Speech not only commits him to the kind of voice he has and to the mode of speech he develops; it also *defines him* as one responded to by those around him with changed diction and attention. They, in turn, expect henceforth to be understood by him with fewer explanations or gestures. Furthermore, a spoken word is a *pact:* there is an irrevocably committing aspect to an utterance remembered by others, although the child may have to learn early that certain commitments (adult ones to a child) are subject to change without notice, while others (his) are not. This intrinsic relationship of speech not only to the world of communicable facts but also to the social value of verbal commitment and uttered truth is strategic among the experiences which support (or fail to support) a sound ego development. It is this psychosocial aspect of the matter which we must learn to relate to the by now better known psychosexual aspects represented, for example, in the autoerotic enjoyment of speech; the use of speech as an erotic "contact"; or in such organ-mode emphases as eliminative or intrusive sounds or uses of speech. Thus the child may come to develop, in the use of voice and word, a particular combination of whining or singing, judging or arguing, as part of a new element of the future identity, namely, the element "one who speaks and is spoken to in such-and-such-a-way." This element, in turn, will be related to other elements of the child's developing identity (he is clever and/or good-looking and/or tough) and will be compared with other people, alive or dead, judged ideal or evil.

It is the ego's function to integrate the psychosexual and psychosocial aspects on a given level of development, and, at the same time, to integrate the relation of newly added identity elements with those already in existence. For earlier crystallizations of identity can become subject to renewed conflict, when changes in the quality and quantity of drive, expansions in mental equipment, and new and often conflicting social demands all make previous adjustments appear insufficient, and, in fact, make previous opportunities and rewards suspect. Yet, such developmental and normative crises differ from imposed, traumatic, and neurotic crises in that the process of growth provides new energy as society offers new and specific opportunities (according to its dominant conception and institutionalization of the phases of life). From a genetic point of view, then, the process of identity formation emerges as an *evolving configuration*—a configuration which is gradually established by successive ego syntheses and resyntheses throughout childhood; it is a configuration gradually integrating *constitutional givens, idiosyncratic libidinal needs, favored capacities, significant identifications, effective defenses, successful sublimations, and consistent roles.*

5

The final assembly of all the converging identity elements at the end of childhood (and the abandonment of the divergent ones)[5] appears to be a formidable task: how can a stage as "abnormal" as adolescence be trusted to accomplish it? Here it is not unnecessary to call to mind again that in spite of the similarity of adolescent "symptoms" and episodes to neurotic and psychotic symptoms and episodes, adolescence is not an affliction but a *normative crisis*, i.e., a normal phase of increased conflict characterized by a seeming fluctuation in ego strength, and yet also by a high growth potential. Neurotic and psychotic crises are defined by a certain self-perpetuating propensity, by an increasing waste of defensive energy, and by a deepened psychosocial isolation; while normative crises are relatively more reversible, or, better, traversable, and are characterized by an abundance of available energy which, to be sure, revives dormant anxiety and arouses new conflict, but also supports new and expanded ego functions in the searching and playful engagement of new opportunities and associations. What under prejudiced scrutiny may appear to be the onset of a neurosis is often but an aggravated crisis which might prove to be self-liquidating and, in fact, contributive to the process of identity formation.

It is true, of course, that the adolescent, during the final stage of his identity formation, is apt to suffer more deeply than he ever did before (or ever will again) from a diffusion of roles; and it is also true that such diffusion renders many an adolescent defenseless against the sudden impact of previously latent malignant disturbances. In the meantime, it is important to emphasize that the diffused and vulnerable, aloof and uncommitted, and yet demanding and opinionated personality of the not-too-neurotic adolescent contains many necessary elements of a semideliberate role experimentation of the "I dare you" and "I dare myself" variety. Much of this apparent diffusion thus must be considered *social play* and thus the true genetic successor of childhood play. Similarly, the adolescent's ego development demands and permits playful, if daring, experimentation in fantasy and *introspection*. We are apt to be alarmed by the "closeness to consciousness" in the adolescent's perception of dangerous id contents (such as the oedipus complex) and this primarily because of the obvious hazards created in psychotherapy, if and when we, in zealous pursuit of our task of "making conscious," push somebody over the precipice of the unconscious who is already leaning out a little too far. The adolescent's leaning out over any number of precipices is normally an experimentation with experiences which are thus becoming more amenable to ego control, provided they can be somehow communicated to other adolescents in one of those strange codes established for just such experiences—and provided they are not prematurely responded to with fatal seriousness by overeager or neurotic adults. The same must be said of the adolescent's "fluidity of defenses," which so often causes raised eyebrows on the part of the worried clinician. Much of this fluidity is anything but pathological; for adolescence is a crisis in which only fluid defense can overcome a sense of victimization by inner and outer demands, and in which only trial and error can lead to the most felicitous avenues of action and self-expression.

In general, one may say that in regard to the social play of adolescents prejudices similar to those which once concerned the nature of childhood play are not easily overcome. We alternately consider such behavior irrelevant, unnecessary, or irrational, and ascribe to it purely regressive and neurotic meanings. As in the past the study of children's spontaneous games was neglected in favor of that of solitary play,[6] so now the mutual "joinedness" of adolescent clique behavior fails to be properly assessed in our concern for the individual adolescent. Children and adolescents in their presocieties provide for one another a sanctioned moratorium and joint support for free experimentation with inner and outer dangers (including those emanating from the adult world). Whether or not a given adolescent's newly acquired capacities are drawn back into infantile conflict depends to a significant extent on the quality of the opportunities and rewards available to him in his peer clique, as well as on the more formal ways in which society at large invites a transition from social play to work experimentation, and from rituals of transit to final commitments: all of which must be based on an implicit mutual contract between the individual and society.

6

Is the sense of identity conscious? At times, of course, it seems only too conscious. For between the double prongs of vital inner need and inexorable outer demand, the still experimenting individual may become the victim of a transitory extreme *identity consciousness* which is the common core of the many forms of "self-consciousness" typical for youth. Where the processes of identity formation are prolonged (a factor which can bring creative gain) such preoccupation with the "self-image" also prevails. We are thus most aware of our identity when we are just about to gain it and when we (with what motion pictures call "a double take") are somewhat surprised to make its acquaintance; or, again, when we are just about to enter a crisis and feel the encroachment of identity diffusion—a syndrome to be described presently.

An increasing sense of identity, on the other hand, is experienced preconsciously as a sense of psychosocial well-being. Its most obvious concomitants are a feeling of being at home in one's body, a sense "knowing where one is going," and an inner assuredness of anticipated recognition from those who count. Such a sense of identity, however, is never gained nor maintained once and for all. Like a "good conscience," it is constantly lost and regained, although more lasting and more economical methods of maintenance and restoration are evolved and fortified in late adolescence.

Like any aspect of well-being or, for that matter, of ego synthesis, a sense of identity has a preconscious aspect which is available to awareness; it expresses itself in behavior which is observable with the naked eye, and it has unconscious concomitants which can be fathomed only by psychological tests and by the psychoanalytic procedure. I regret that, at this point, I can bring forward only a general claim which awaits detailed demonstration. The claim advanced here concerns a whole series of criteria of psychosocial health which find their specific elaboration and relative completion in stages of development preceding and following the identity crisis. This is condensed in Figure III.

Identity appears as only one concept within a wider conception of the human life cycle which envisages childhood as a *gradual unfolding of the personality through phase-specific psychosocial crises:* I have, on other occasions (1950a, 1950b), expressed this *epigenetic principle* by taking recourse to a diagram which, with its many empty boxes, at intervals may serve as a check on our attempts at detailing psychosocial development. (Such a diagram, however, can be recommended to the serious attention only of those who can take it *and* leave it.) The diagram (Figure III), at first, contained only the double-lined boxes along the descending diagonal (I, 1; II, 2; III, 3; IV, 4; V, 5; VI, 6; VII, 7; VIII, 8) and for the sake of initial orientation, the reader is requested to ignore all other entries for the moment. The *diagonal* shows the sequence of psychosocial crises. Each of these boxes is shared by a criterion of relative psychosocial health and the corresponding criterion of relative psychosocial ill-health: in "normal" development, the first must persistently outweigh (although it will never completely do away with) the second. The sequence of stages thus represents a

	1	2	3	4	5	6	7	8
I INFANCY	Trust vs. Mistrust				Unipolarity vs. Premature Self-differentiation			
II EARLY CHILDHOOD		Autonomy vs. Shame, Doubt			Bipolarity vs. Autism			
III PLAY AGE			Initiative vs. Guilt		Play Identification vs. (Oedipal) Fantasy Identities			
IV SCHOOL AGE				Industry vs. Inferiority	Work Identification vs. Identity Foreclosure			
V ADOLESCENCE	Time Perspective vs. Time Diffusion	Self-certainty vs. Identity Consciousness	Role Experimentation vs. Negative Identity	Anticipation of Achievement vs. Work Paralysis	Identity vs. Identity Diffusion	Sexual Identity vs. Bisexual Diffusion	Leadership Polarization vs. Authority Diffusion	Ideological Polarization vs. Diffusion of Ideals
VI YOUNG ADULT					Solidarity vs. Social Isolation	Intimacy vs. Isolation		
VII ADULTHOOD							Generativity vs. Self-absorption	
VIII MATURE AGE								Integrity vs. Disgust, Despair

Figure III

successive development of the component parts of the psychosocial personality. Each part exists in some form (verticals) before the time when it becomes "phase-specific," i.e., when "its" psychosocial crisis is precipitated both by the individual's readiness and by society's pressure. But each component comes to ascendance and finds its more or less lasting solution at the conclusion of "its" stage. It is thus *systematically related* to all the others, and all depend on the proper development at the proper *time* of each; although individual make-up and the nature of society determine the rate of development of each of them, and thus the *ratio* of all of them. It is at the end of adolescence, then, that identity becomes phase-specific (V, 5), i.e., must find a certain integration as a relatively conflict-free psychosocial arrangement—or remain defective or conflict-laden.

With this chart as a blueprint before us, let me state first which aspects of this complex matter will *not* be treated in this paper: for one, we will not be able to make more definitive the now very tentative designation (in vertical 5) of the precursors of identity in the infantile ego. Rather we approach childhood in an untraditional manner, namely, from young adulthood backward—and this with the conviction that early development cannot be understood on its own terms alone, and that the earliest stages of childhood cannot be accounted for without a unified theory of the whole span of preadulthood. For the infant (while he is not spared the chaos of needful rage) does not and cannot build anew and out of himself the course of human life, as the reconstruction of his earliest experience ever again seems to suggest. The smallest child lives in a community of life cycles which depend on him as he depends on them, and which guide his drives as well as his sublimations with consistent feedbacks. This verity necessitates a discussion of the psychoanalytic approach to "environment" to which we shall return toward the end of this paper.

A second systematic omission concerns the psychosexual stages. Those readers who have undertaken to study the diagrams of psychosexual development in *Childhood and Society* (Erikson,

1950a) know that I am attempting to lay the ground for a detailed account of the dovetailing of psychosexual and psychosocial epigenesis, i.e., the two schedules according to which component parts, present throughout development, come to fruition in successive stages. The essential inseparability of these two schedules is implied throughout this paper, although only the psychosocial schedule, and in fact only one stage of it, is brought into focus.

What traditional source of psychoanalytic insight, then, *will* we concern ourselves with? It is: first pathography; in this case the clinical description of *identity confusion*. Hoping thus to clarify the matter of identity from a more familiar angle, we will then return to the over-all aim of beginning to "extract," as Freud put it, "from psychopathology what may be of benefit to normal psychology."

PATHOGRAPHIC: THE CLINICAL PICTURE OF IDENTITY CONFUSION

Pathography remains the traditional source of psychoanalytic insight. In the following, I shall sketch a syndrome of disturbances in young people who can neither make use of the institutionalized moratorium provided in their society, nor create and maintain for themselves (as Shaw did) a unique moratorium all of their own. They come, instead, to psychiatrists, priests, judges, and (we must add) recruitment officers in order to be given an authorized if ever so uncomfortable place in which to wait things out.

The sources at my disposal are the case histories of a number of young patients who sought treatment following an acutely disturbed period between the ages of sixteen and twenty-four. A few were seen, and fewer treated, by me personally; a larger number were reported in supervisory interviews or seminars at the Austen Riggs Center in Stockbridge and at the Western Psychiatric Institute in Pittsburgh; the largest number are former patients now on record in the files of the Austen Riggs Center. My *composite sketch* of these case histories will remind the reader immediately of the diagnostic and technical problems encountered in adolescents in general (Blos, 1953) and especially in any number of those young borderline cases (Knight, 1953) who are customarily diagnosed as preschizophrenias, or severe character disorders with paranoid, depressive, psychopathic, or other trends. Such well-established diagnostic signposts will not be questioned here. An attempt will be made, however, to concentrate on certain common features representative of the common life crisis shared by this whole group of patients as a result of a (temporary or final) inability of their egos to establish an identity: for they all suffer from *acute identity confusion*. [7] Obviously, only quite detailed case presentations could convey the full necessity or advisability of such a "phase-specific" approach which emphasizes the life task shared by a group of patients as much as the diagnostic criteria which differentiate them. In the meantime, I hope that my composite sketch will convey at least a kind of impressionistic plausibility. The fact that the cases known to me were seen in a private institution in the Berkshires and at a public clinic in industrial Pittsburgh, suggests that at least the two extremes of socioeconomic status in the United States (and thus two extreme forms of identity problems) are represented here. This could mean that the families in question, because of their extreme locations on the scale of class mobility and of Americanization, may have conveyed to these particular children a certain hopelessness regarding their chances of participating in (or of successfully defying) the dominant American manners and symbols of success. [8] Whether, and in what way, disturbances such as are outlined here also characterize those more comfortably placed somewhere near the middle of the socioeconomic ladder, remains, at this time, an open question.

Time of Breakdown

A state of acute identity confusion usually becomes manifest at a time when the young individual finds himself exposed to a combination of experiences which demand his simultaneous commitment to *physical intimacy* (not by any means always overtly sexual), to decisive *occupational choice*, to energetic *competition*, and to *psychosocial self-definition*. A young college girl, previously overprotected by a conservative mother who is trying to live down a not-so-conservative past, may, on entering college, meet young people of radically different backgrounds, among whom she must choose her friends and her enemies; radically different mores especially in the relationship of the sexes which she must play along with or repudiate; and a commitment to make decisions and choices which will necessitate irreversible competitive involvement or even leadership. Often she finds among very "different" young people a comfortable display of values, manners, and symbols for which one or the other of her parents or grandparents is covertly nostalgic, while overtly despising them. Decisions and choices and, most of all, successes in any direction bring to the fore conflicting identifications and immediately threaten to narrow down the inventory of further tentative choices; and, at the very moment when time is of the essence, every move may establish a binding precedent in psychosocial self-definition, i.e., in the "type" one comes to represent in the types of the age-mates (who seem so terribly eager to type). On the other hand, any marked *avoidance of choices* (i.e., a moratorium by default) leads to a sense of outer *isolation* and to an *inner vacuum* which is wide open for old libidinal objects and with this for bewilderingly conscious incestuous feelings; for more primitive forms of identification; and (in some) for a renewed struggle with archaic introjects. This regressive pull often receives the greatest attention from workers in our field, partially because we are on more familiar ground wherever we can discern signs of regression to infantile psychosexuality. Yet the disturbances under discussion here cannot be comprehended without some insight into the specific nature of transitory adolescent regression as an attempt to postpone and to avoid, as it were, a psychosocial foreclosure. A state of paralysis may ensue, the mechanisms of which appear to be devised to maintain a state of minimal actual choice and commitment with a maximum inner conviction of still being the chooser. Of the complicated presenting pathology only a few aspects can be discussed here.

The Problem of Intimacy

The chart which accompanied the preceding section shows "Intimacy vs. Isolation" as the core conflict which follows that of "Identity vs. Identity Diffusion." That many of our patients break down at an age which is properly considered more preadult than postadolescent is explained by the fact that often only an attempt to engage in intimate fellowship and competition or in sexual intimacy fully reveals the latent weakness of identity.

True "engagement" with others is the result and the test of firm self-delineation. Where this is still missing, the young individual, when seeking tentative forms of playful intimacy in friendship and competition, in sex play and love, in argument and gossip, is apt to experience a peculiar strain, as if such tentative engagement might turn into an interpersonal fusion amounting to a loss of identity, and requiring, therefore, a tense inner reservation, a caution in commitment. Where a youth does not resolve such strain he may isolate himself and enter, at best, only stereotyped and formalized interpersonal relations; or he may, in repeated hectic attempts and repeated dismal failures, seek intimacy with the most improbable partners. For where an assured sense of identity is missing, even friendships and affairs become desperate attempts at delineating the fuzzy outlines of identity by mutual narcissistic mirroring: to fall in love then often means to fall into one's mirror image, hurting oneself and damaging the mirror. During lovemaking or in sexual fantasies, a loosening of *sexual identity* threatens: it even becomes unclear whether sexual excitement is experienced by the individual or by his partner, and this in either heterosexual or homosexual encounters. The ego thus loses its flexible capacity for abandoning itself to sexual and affectual sensations, in a fusion with another individual who is both partner to the sensation and guarantor of one's continuing identity: fusion with another becomes identity loss. A sudden collapse of all capacity for mutuality threatens, and a desperate wish ensues to start all over again, with a (quasi-deliberate) regression to a stage of basic bewilderment and rage such as only the very small child knows.

It must be remembered that the counterpart of intimacy is *distantiation*, i.e., the readiness to repudiate, to ignore, or to destroy those forces and people whose essence seems dangerous to one's own. Intimacy with one set of people and ideas would not be really intimate without an efficient repudiation of another set. Thus, weakness or excess in repudiation is an intrinsic aspect of the inability to gain intimacy because of an incomplete identity: whoever is not sure of this "point of view" cannot repudiate judiciously.

Young persons often indicate in rather pathetic ways a feeling that only a merging with a "leader" can save them—an adult who is able and willing to offer himself as a safe object for experimental surrender and as a guide in the relearning of the very first steps toward an intimate mutuality, and a legitimate repudiation. To such a person the late adolescent wants to be an apprentice or a disciple, a follower, sex mate or patient. Where this fails, as it often must from its very intensity and absoluteness, the young individual recoils to a position of strenuous introspection and self-testing which, given particularly aggravating circumstances or a history of relatively strong autistic trends, can lead him into a paralyzing borderline state. Symptomatically, this state consists of a painfully heightened sense of isolation; a disintegration of the sense of inner continuity and sameness; a sense of over-all ashamedness; an inability to derive a sense of accomplishment from any kind of activity; a feeling that life is happening to the individual rather than being lived by his initiative; a radically shortened time perspective; and finally, a basic mistrust, which leaves it to the world, to society, and indeed to psychiatry to prove that the patient does exist in a psychosocial sense, i.e., can count on an invitation to become himself.

Diffusion of Time Perspective

In extreme instances of delayed and prolonged adolescence an extreme form of a disturbance in the *experience of time* appears which, in its milder form, belongs to the psychopathology of everyday adolescence. It consists of a sense of great urgency and yet also of a loss of consideration for time as a dimension of living. The young person may feel simultaneously very young, and in fact babylike, and old beyond rejuvenation. Protests of missed greatness and of a premature and fatal loss of useful potentials are common among our patients as they are among adolescents in cultures which consider such protestations romantic; the implied malignancy, however, consists of a decided disbelief in the possibility that time may bring change, and yet also of a violent fear that it might. This contradiction often is expressed in a general slowing up which makes the patient behave, within the routine of activities (and also of therapy) as if he were moving in molasses. It is hard for him to go to bed and to face the transition into a state of sleep, and it is equally hard for him to get up and face the necessary restitution of wakefulness; it is hard to come to the hour, and hard to leave it. Such complaints as, "I don't know," "I give up," "I quit," are by no means mere habitual statements reflecting a mild depression: they are often expressions of the kind of despair which Edward Bibring (1953) has recently discussed as a wish on the part of the ego "to let itself die." The assumption that life could actually be made to end with the end of adolescence (or at tentatively planned later "dates of expiration") is by no means entirely unwelcome, and, in fact, can become the only pillar of hope on which a new beginning can be based. Some of our patients even require the feeling that the therapist does not intend to commit them to a continuation of life if (successful) treatment should fail to prove it really worth while; without such a conviction the moratorium would not be a real one. In the meantime, the "wish to die" is only in those rare cases a really suicidal wish, where "to be a suicide" becomes an inescapable identity choice in itself. I am thinking here of a pretty young girl, the oldest of a number of daughters of a millworker. Her mother had repeatedly expressed the thought that she would rather see her daughters dead than become prostitutes; at the same time she suspected "prostitution" in their every move toward companionship with boys. The daughters were finally forced into a kind of conspiratorial sorority of their own, obviously designed to elude the mother, to experiment with ambiguous situations, and yet probably also to give one another protection from men. They were finally caught in compromising circumstances. The authorities, too, took it for granted that they intended to prostitute themselves, and they were sent to a variety of institutions where they were forcefully impressed with the kind of "recognition" society had in store for them. No appeal was possible to a mother who, they felt, had left them no choice; and much good will and understanding of social workers was sabotaged by circumstances. At least for the oldest girl (and this, because of a number of reasons) no other future was available except that of another chance in another world. She killed herself by hanging after having dressed herself up nicely, and having written a note which ended with the cryptic words "Why I achieve honor only to discard it. . . ."

Less spectacular but not less malignant forms and origins of such "negative identities" will be taken up later.

Diffusion of Industry

Cases of severe identity diffusion regularly also suffer from an acute upset in the sense of workmanship, and this either in the form of an inability to concentrate on required or suggested tasks, or in a self-destructive preoccupation with some one-sided activities, e.g., excessive reading. The way in which such patients sometimes, under treatment, find the one activity in which they can re-employ their once lost sense of workmanship is a chapter in itself. Here, it is well to keep in mind the stage of development which precedes puberty and adolescence, namely, the elementary-school age, when the child is taught the prerequisites for participation in the particular technology of his culture and is given the opportunity and the life task of developing a sense of workmanship and work participation. The school age significantly follows the oedipal stage: the accomplishment of real (and not only playful) steps toward a place in the economic structure of society permits the child to reidentify with parents as workers and tradition bearers rather than as sexual and familial beings, thus nurturing at least one concrete and more "neutral" possibility of becoming like them. The tangible goals of elementary practice are shared by and with age-mates in places of instruction (sweathouse, prayer house, fishing hole, workshop, kitchen, schoolhouse) most of which, in turn, are geographically separated from the home, from the mother, and from infantile memories: here, however, wide differences in the treatment of the sexes exist. Work goals, then, by no means only support or exploit the suppression of infantile instinctual aims; they also enhance the functioning of the ego, in that they offer a constructive activity with actual tools and materials in a communal reality. The ego's tendency to turn passivity into activity here thus acquires a new field of manifestation, in many ways superior to the mere turning of passive into active in infantile fantasy and play; for now the inner need for activity, practice, and work completion is ready to meet the corresponding demands and opportunities in social reality (Hendrick, 1943; Ginsburg, 1954).

Because of the immediate oedipal antecedents of the beginnings of a work identity, the diffusion of identity in our young patients reverses their gears toward oedipal competitiveness and sibling rivalry. Thus identity diffusion is accompanied not only by an inability to concentrate, but also by an excessive awareness as well as an abhorrence of competitiveness. Although the patients in question usually are intelligent and able and often have shown themselves successful in office work, in scholastic studies, and in sports, they now lose the capacity for work, exercise, and sociability, and thus the most important vehicle of social play, and the most significant refuge from formless fantasy and vague anxiety. Instead infantile goals and fantasies are dangerously endowed with the energy emanating from matured sexual equipment and increased aggressive power. One parent, again, becomes the goal, the other, again, the hindrance. Yet this revived oedipal struggle is not and must not be interpreted as exclusively or even primarily a sexual one: it is a turn toward the earliest origins, an attempt to resolve a diffusion of early introjects and to rebuild shaky childhood identifications—in other words, a wish to be born again, to learn once more the very first steps toward reality and mutuality, and to acquire the renewed permission to develop again the functions of contact, activity, and competition.

A young patient, who had found himself blocked in college, during the initial phase of his treatment in a private hospital nearly read himself blind, apparently in a destructive overidentification with father and therapist, both of whom were professors. Guided by a resourceful "painter in residence" he came upon the fact that he had an original and forceful talent to paint, an activity which was prevented by advancing treatment from becoming self-destructive overactivity. As painting proved a help in the patient's gradual acquisition of a sense of identity of his own, he dreamed one night a different version of a dream which previously had always ended in panicky awakening. Now he fled, from fire and persecution, into a forest which he had sketched himself; and as he fled into it, the charcoal drawing turned into live woods, with an infinite perspective.

The Choice of the Negative Identity

The loss of a sense of identity often is expressed in a scornful and snobbish hostility toward the roles offered as proper and desirable by one's family or immediate community. Any part aspect of the required role, or all parts, be it masculinity or femininity, nationality or class membership, can become the main focus of the young person's acid disdain. Such excessive contempt for their backgrounds occurs among the oldest Anglo-Saxon and the newest Latin or Jewish families; it easily becomes a general dislike for everything American, and an irrational overestimation of everything foreign. Life and strength seem to exist only where one is not, while decay and danger threaten wherever one happens to be. This typical case fragment illustrates the superego's triumph of depreciation over a young man's faltering identity: "A voice within him which was disparaging him began to increase at about this time. It went to the point of intruding into everything he did. He said, 'If I smoke a cigarette, if I tell a girl I like her, if I make a gesture, if I listen to music, if I try to read a book—this third voice is at me all the time—"You're doing this for effect; you're a phony." ' This disparaging voice in the last year has been rather relentless. The other day on the way from home to college, getting into New York on the train, he went through some of the New Jersey swamplands and the poorer sections of the cities, and he felt that he was more congenial with people who lived there than he was with people on the campus or at home. He felt that life really existed in those places and that the campus was a sheltered, effeminate place."

In this example it is important to recognize not only an over-weening superego, overclearly perceived as an inner voice, but also the acute identity diffusion, as projected on segments of society. An analogous case is that of a French-American girl from a rather prosperous mining town, who felt panicky to the point of paralysis when alone with a boy. It appeared that numerous superego injunctions and identity conflicts had, as it were, short-circuited in the obsessive idea that every boy had a right to expect from her a yielding to sexual practices popularly designated as "French."

Such estrangement from national and ethnic origins rarely leads to a complete denial of *personal identity* (Piers and Singer, 1953), although the angry insistence on being called by a particular given name or nickname is not uncommon among young people who try to find a refuge from diffusion in a new name label. Yet confabulatory reconstructions of one's origin do occur: a high-school girl of Middle-European descent secretly kept company with Scottish immigrants, carefully studying and easily assimilating their dialect and their social habits. With the help of history books and travel guides she reconstructed for herself a childhood in a given milieu in an actual township in Scotland, apparently convincing enough to some descendants of that country. Prevailed upon to discuss her future with me, she spoke of her (American-born) parents as "the people who brought me over here," and told me of her childhood "over there" in impressive detail. I went along with the story, implying that it had more inner truth than reality to it. The bit of reality was, as I surmised, the girl's attachment, in early childhood, to a woman neighbor who had come from the British Isles; the force behind the near-delusional "truth" was the paranoid form of a powerful death wish (latent in all severe identity crises) against her parents. The semideliberateness of the delusion was indicated when I finally asked the girl how she had managed to marshal all the details of life in Scotland. "Bless you, sir," she said in pleading Scottish brogue, "I needed a past."

On the whole, however, our patients' conflicts find expression in a more subtle way than the abrogation of personal identity: they rather choose a *negative identity*, i.e., an identity perversely based on all those identifications and roles which, at critical stages of development, had been presented to the individual as most undesirable or dangerous, and yet also as most real. For example, a mother whose first-born son died and who (because of complicated guilt feelings) has never been able to attach to her later surviving children the same amount of religious devotion that she bestows on the memory of her dead child may well arouse in one of her sons the conviction that to be sick or dead is a better assurance of being "recognized" than to be healthy and about. A mother who is filled with unconscious ambivalence toward a brother who disintegrated into alcoholism may again and again respond selectively only to those traits in her son which seem to point to a repetition of her brother's fate, in which case this "negative" identity may take on more reality for the son than all his natural attempts at being good: he may work hard on becoming a drunkard and, lacking the necessary ingredients, may end up in a state of stubborn paralysis of choice. In other cases the negative identity is dictated by the necessity of finding and defending a niche of one's own against the excessive ideals either demanded by morbidly ambitious parents or seemingly already realized by actually superior ones: in both cases the parents' weaknesses and unexpressed wishes are recognized by the child with catastrophic clarity. The daughter of a man of brilliant showmanship ran away from college and was arrested as a prostitute in the Negro quarter of a Southern city; while the daughter of an influential Southern Negro preacher was found among narcotic addicts in Chicago. In such cases it is of utmost importance to recognize the mockery and the vindictive pretense in such role playing; for the white girl had not really prostituted herself, and the colored girl had not really become an addict—yet. Needless to say, however, each of them had put herself into a marginal social area, leaving it to law-enforcement officers and to psychiatric agencies to decide what stamp to put on such behavior. A corresponding case is that of a boy presented to a psychiatric clinic as "the village homosexual" of a small town. On investigation, it appeared that the boy had succeeded in assuming this fame without any actual acts of homosexuality except one, much earlier in his life, when he had been raped by some older boys.

Such vindictive choices of a negative identity represent, of course, a desperate attempt at regaining some mastery in a situation in which the available positive identity elements cancel each other out. The history of such a choice reveals a set of conditions in which it is easier to derive a sense of identity out of a *total* identification with that which one is *least* supposed to be than to struggle for a feeling of reality in acceptable roles which are unattainable with the patient's inner means. The statement of a young man, "I would rather be quite insecure than a little secure," and that of a young woman, "At least in the gutter I'm a genius," circumscribe the relief following the total choice of a negative identity. Such relief is, of course, often sought collectively in cliques and gangs of young homosexuals, addicts, and social cynics.

A relevant job ahead of us is the analysis of snobbism which, in its upper-class form, permits some people to deny their identity diffusion through a recourse to something they did not earn themselves, namely, their parents' wealth, background, or fame. But there is a "lower lower" snobbism too, which is based on the pride of having achieved a semblance of nothingness. At any rate, many a late adolescent, if faced with continuing diffusion, would rather *be nobody or somebody bad, and this totally, or indeed, dead— by free choice—than be not-quite-somebody.* The word "total" is not accidental in this connection, for I have endeavored to describe in another connection (Erikson, 1953) a human proclivity to a "totalistic" reorientation when, at critical stages of development, reintegration into a relative "wholeness" seems impossible.[9] We will return to this problem in the last section.

Transference and Resistance

What I can say here about the therapeutic problems encountered with the patients described must be restricted to an attempt at relating to the concepts of identity and diffusion such matters of therapeutic technique as have been elaborated by workers in the field of borderline cases.[10]

On facing therapy, some of the patients under discussion here undergo a phase of particular malignancy. While the depth of regression and the danger of acting out must of course guide our diagnostic decisions, it is important to recognize, from the start, a mechanism present in such a turn for the worse: I would call it the "rock-bottom attitude." This consists of a quasi-deliberate giving in on the part of the patient to the pull of regression, a radical search for the rock bottom—i.e., both the ultimate limit of regression and the only firm foundation for a renewed progression.[11]

The assumption of such a deliberate search for the "base line" means to carry Ernst Kris's "regression in the service of the ego" to an extreme: the fact that the recovery of our patients sometimes coincides with the discovery of previously hidden artistic gifts suggests further study of this point (Kris, 1952).

The element of deliberateness added here to "true" regression is often expressed in an all-pervasive mockery which characterizes the initial therapeutic contact with these patients; and by that strange air of sadomasochistic satisfaction, which makes it often hard to see and harder to believe that their self-depreciation and their willingness to "let the ego die" harbors a devastating sincerity. As one patient said: "That people do not know how to succeed is bad enough. But the worst is that they do not know how to fail. I have decided to fail well." This almost "deadly" sincerity is to be found in the patients' very determination to *trust nothing but mistrust*, and yet to watch from a dark corner of their minds (and indeed, often from the corner of an eye) for new experiences simple and forthright enough to permit a renewal of the most basic experiments in trustful mutuality. The therapist, manifestly faced with a mocking and defiant young adult, actually must take over the task of a mother who introduces a baby to life's trustworthiness. In the center of the treatment is the patient's need to redelineate himself, and thus to rebuild the foundations of his identity. At the beginning these delineations shift abruptly, even as violent shifts in the patient's experience of his ego boundary take place before our eyes: the patient's mobility may suddenly undergo a "catatonic" slowdown; his attentiveness may turn into overwhelming sleepiness; his vasomotor system may overreact to the point of producing sensations of fainting; his sense of reality may yield to feelings of depersonalization; or the remnants of his self-assurance may disappear in a miasmic loss of a sense of physical presence. Cautious but firm inquiry will reveal the probability that a number of contradictory impulses preceded the "attack." There is first a sudden intense impulse completely to destroy the therapist, and this, it seems, with an underlying "cannibalistic" wish to devour his essence and his identity. At the

same time, or in alternation, there occur a fear and a wish to be
devoured, to gain an identity by being absorbed in the therapist's
essence. Both tendencies, of course, are often dissimulated or
somatized for long periods, during which they find a manifestation (often kept secret) only after the therapeutic hour. This
manifestation may be an impulsive flight into sexual promiscuity
acted out without sexual satisfaction or any sense of participation;
enormously absorbing rituals of masturbation or food intake;
excessive drinking or wild driving; or self-destructive marathons
of reading or listening to music, without food or sleep.

We see here the most extreme form of what may be called
identity resistance, which, incidentally, far from being restricted to
the patients described here, is a universal form of resistance
regularly experienced but often unrecognized in the course of
analyses. Identity resistance is, in its milder and more usual
forms, the patient's fear that the analyst, because of his particular
personality, background, or philosophy, may carelessly or deliberately destroy the weak core of the patient's identity and impose
instead his own. I would not hesitate to say that some of the
much-discussed unsolved transference neuroses in patients, as
well as in candidates in training, are the direct result of the fact
that the identity resistance often is, at best, analyzed only quite
unsystematically. In such cases the analysand may throughout
the analysis resist any possible inroad by the analyst's identity
while surrendering on all other points; or he may absorb more of
the analyst's identity than is manageable within the patient's own
means; or he may leave the analysis with a lifelong sense of not
having been provided with some essence owed to him by the
analyst.

In cases of acute identity diffusion this identity resistance
becomes the core problem of the therapeutic encounter. Variations of psychoanalytic technique have in common that the dominant resistance must be accepted as the main guide to technique
and that interpretation must be fitted to the patient's ability to
utilize it. Here the patient sabotages communication until he has
settled some basic—if contradictory—issues. The patient insists

that the therapist accept his negative identity as real and necessary (which it is and was) without concluding that this negative identity is "all there is to him." If the therapist is able to fulfill both of these demands, he must prove patiently through many severe crises that he can maintain understanding and affection for the patient without either devouring him or offering himself for a totem meal. Only then can better known forms of transference, if ever so reluctantly, emerge.

These are nothing more than a few hints regarding the phenomenology of identity confusion as reflected in the most outstanding and immediate transferences and resistances. Individual treatment, however, is only one facet of therapy in the cases under discussion. The transferences of these patients remain diffused, while their acting out remains a constant danger. Some, therefore, need to undergo treatment in a hospital environment in which their stepping out of the therapeutic relationship can be observed and limited; and in which first steps *beyond* the newly won bipolar relationship to the therapist meet with the immediate support of receptive nurses, cooperative fellow patients, and helpful instructors in a sufficiently wide choice of activities.

Specific Factors in Family and Childhood

In the discussion of patients who have a relevant pathogenic trend in common, we are apt to ask what their parents have in common. I think that one may say that a number of the mothers in our case histories have in common some outstanding traits. The first is a pronounced status awareness, of the climbing and pretentious or of the "hold-on" variety. They would at almost any time be willing to overrule matters of honest feeling and of intelligent judgment for the sake of a façade of wealth, propriety, and "happiness": they, in fact, try to coerce their sensitive children into a pretense of a "natural" and "glad-to-be-proper" sociability. They also have the special quality of a penetrating omnipresence; their very voices and their softest sobs are sharp, plaintive, or fretful, and cannot be escaped within a considerable radius. One patient, all through childhood had a repetitive dream of a pair of flapping scissors flying around a room: the scissors proved to symbolize his mother's voice, cutting, and cutting off.[12] These mothers love, but they love fearfully, plaintively, instrusively; they are themselves so hungry for approval and for recognition that they burden their young children with complicated complaints, especially about the father, and they plead with the children to justify by their existence their mother's existence. They are highly jealous and highly sensitive to the jealousy of others; in our context it is especially important that the mother is intensely jealous of any sign that the child may identify primarily with the father, or, worse, base his very identity on that of the father. It must be added that whatever these mothers are, they are more so toward the patient; the conclusion is inescapable that these patients, in turn, have, from the beginning, deeply hurt their mothers by shying away from them, and this because of an utter intolerance of extreme temperamental differences. These differences, however, are only extreme expressions of an essential affinity: by which I mean to imply that the patient's excessive tendency to withdraw (or to act impulsively) and the mother's excessive social intrusiveness have in common a high degree of social vulnerability. Behind the mother's persistent complaints, then, that the father failed to make a woman out of her, is the complaint, deeply perceived by both mother and child, that the patient failed to make a mother out of her.

The fathers, while usually successful, and often outstanding in their particular fields, do not stand up against their wives at home because of an excessive mother dependence on them, in consequence of which the fathers also are deeply jealous of their children. What initiative and integrity they have either surrenders to the wife's intrusiveness or tries guiltily to elude her: in consequence of which the mother becomes only the more needy, plaintive, and "sacrificial" in her demands upon all or some of her children.

Of the relationship of our patients to their brothers and sisters I can only say that it seems to be more symbiotic than most sibling relationships are. Because of an early identity hunger, our patients are apt to attach themselves to one brother or sister in a way resembling the behavior of twins (Burlingham, 1952), except that here we have one twin, as it were, trying to treat a nontwin as a twin. They seem apt to surrender to a total identification with at least one sibling in ways which go far beyond the "altruism by identification" described by Anna Freud (1936). It is as if our patients surrendered their own identity to that of a brother or sister in the hope of regaining a bigger and better one by some act of merging. For periods they succeed; the letdown which must follow the breakup of the artificial twinship is only the more traumatic. Rage and paralysis follow the sudden insight that there is enough identity only for one, and that the other seems to have made off with it.

The early childhood histories of our patients are, on the whole, remarkably bland. Some infantile autism is often observed early but usually rationalized by the parents. Yet one has the general impression that the degree of malignancy of the acute identity confusion in late adolescence depends on the extent of this early autism, which will determine the depth of regression and the intensity of the encounter between new identity fragments and old introjects. As to particular traumata in childhood or youth, one item seems frequent, namely, a severe physical trauma either in the oedipal period or in early puberty—and this in connection with a separation from home. This trauma may consist of an operation or a belatedly diagnosed physical defect; it may be an accident or a severe sexual traumatization. Otherwise the early pathology conforms with that expected as typical for the dominant psychiatric diagnosis given.

The Therapeutic Design

I promised a composite sketch, and a sketch I have presented. Again, only the detailed presentation of a few cases could elucidate the relation of ego weakness to congenital proclivities, on the one hand, and to the educative deficiency of families and classes, on the other. In the meantime, the most immediate clarification of the ego's relationship to its "environment" ensues from the study of the young patient's recovery in a hospital setting, i.e., the study of his determined "oneliness" (as a young woman patient put it); of his tendency to exploit and provoke the hospital environment; of his growing ability to utilize it; and finally, of his capacity to leave this kind of institutionalized moratorium and to return to his old or new place in society. The hospital community offers the clinical researcher the possibility of being a participant observer not only in the individual patient's personal treatment but also in the "therapeutic design" which is to meet the legitimate demands of patients who share a life problem—here identity diffusion. It stands to reason that a typical problem receives elucidation as the hospital community studies what is required to treat a particular age group: in this case the hospital becomes a planfully institutionalized world-between-worlds, which offers the young individual support in the rebuilding of those most vital ego functions, which—as far as he ever built them—he has relinquished. The relationship to the individual therapist is the cornerstone for the establishment of a new and honest mutuality of function which must set the patient's face toward an ever so dimly perceived and ever so strenuously refuted future. Yet, it is the hospital community in which the patient's first steps of renewed social experimentation take place. The privileges and obligations of such a community immediately demand his subjection to and his initiation in a communal design which will also strive to meet his and his fellow patients' needs—and incidentally, also, those of the staff: for it stands to reason that a communal setting such as a hospital is characterized not only by the identity needs of those who happen to be the patients, but also of those who choose to become their brothers' (and sisters') keepers. The discussion of the ways in which the professional hierarchy distributes the functions, the rewards, and the status of such keepership (and thus opens the door for a variety of countertransferences and "crosstransferences" which, indeed, make the hospital a facsimile of a home) is entering the literature on the subject of hospital morale (i.e., Bateman and Dunham, 1948; Schwartz and Will, 1953). From the point of view of this paper, such studies also clearly point to the danger of the patient's choosing the very role of a patient as the basis of his crystallizing identity: for this role may well prove more meaningful than any potential identity experienced before (see K. T. Erikson, 1957).

Once More: The Diagram

Diagrams have a quiet coerciveness all their own. Especially does a diagram which has neither been completed nor discarded become a conceptual ghost: one converses with it unawares. In therapeutic work, one tries to ignore the embarrassing fact that now and again the diagram looks over one's shoulder, as it were, and makes a suggestion; nor do the patients appreciate such atmospheric interferences. Only as I concluded this impressionistic survey of some of the main features of identity diffusion, did it occur to me to "locate" them on the chart: and it cannot be denied that they clarify previously vague parts of the diagram and suggest specific expansions of theory. Insisting, then, that in principle ghosts should remain expendable, we will briefly outline what this one can teach us.

The original chart showed only the diagonal, i.e., the successive achievement (or failure) of the main components of relative psychosocial health. However, it bore the legend: "Above the diagonal there is space for a future elaboration of the precursors of each of these solutions, all of which begin with the beginning; below the diagonal there is space for the designation of the derivatives of these solutions in the maturing personality."

Because all the *verticals* "begin with the beginning," one hesitates to enter even tentative terms into the top boxes. Yet, work with borderline cases (adolescent, juvenile, and infantile) suggests that the infantile frontier, to which they have all regressed, is that of a basic mistrust in their *self-delineation* and of a basic doubt in the possibility of any relationship of *mutuality*. The chart, tentatively, assumes that a successful struggle on the earliest psychosocial frontier of infancy (i.e., the *Trust–Mistrust* frontier), if well guided by a favorable maternal environment, leads to a dominant sense of *Unipolarity* (I, 5), by which is meant something like a dominant sense of the goodness of individual existence. This, I believe, deserves to be differentiated from the narcissistic omnipotence ascribed to this age. While still vulnerably dependent on direct, continuous, and consistent maternal support, an actual sense of the reality of "good" powers, outside and within oneself, must be assumed to arise. Its negative counterpart is a diffusion of contradictory introjects and a predominance of fantasies which pretend to coerce hostile reality with omnipotent vengeance. Once gained, however, the psychosocial foundation of unipolarity subsequently permits *Bipolarization* (II, 5) or what, in id terms, has been called the cathexis of objects. This permits an outgoing experimentation with powerful but loving individuals who retain consistent reality, even though they may go before they come, deny before they give, seem indifferent before they again become attentive. In transitory or lasting forms of autism, the child can be seen to shy away from or to despair of such bipolarization, always in search of an illusory safe "oneliness."

Subsequent *Play* and *Work Identifications* (III, 5—IV, 5) with powerful adults and with older and younger age-mates need no further discussion here; the literature on the preschool and school stage amply illustrates the gains and the defeats of these more obviously psychosocial periods.

It is horizontal V which contains the *derivatives of earlier relative achievements which now become part and parcel of the struggle for identity*. It is necessary to emphasize (and possible to illustrate briefly) the principle according to which early relative achievements (diagonal) when considered at a later stage (any horizontal below the diagonal) must be reviewed and renamed in terms of that later stage. Basic *Trust*, for example, is a good and a most fundamental thing to have, but its psychosocial quality becomes more differentiated as the ego comes into the possession of a more extensive apparatus, even as society challenges and guides such extension.

To begin, then, with the pathology just described: *Time Diffusion* (V, 1) or a loss of the ego's function of maintaining perspective and expectancy is related to the *earliest crises in life* (I, 1), and this because of the fact that the conception of temporal cycles and of time qualities is inherent in and develops from the first experience of mounting need tension, of delay of satisfaction, and final unification with the satisfying "object." As tension increases, future fulfillment is anticipated in "hallucinatory" images; as fulfillment is delayed, moments of impotent rage occur in which anticipation (and with it, future) is obliterated; the perception of an approaching potential satisfaction again gives time a highly condensed quality of intense hope and feared disappointment. All of this contributes temporal elements to the formation of basic trust, i.e., the inner conviction that—after all—sufficient satisfaction is sufficiently predictable to make waiting and "working" worth while. Whatever the original inventory of time qualities are, our most malignantly regressed young people are clearly possessed by general attitudes which represent something of a mistrust of time as such: every delay appears to be a deceit, every wait an experience of impotence, every hope a danger, every plan a catastrophe, every potential provider a traitor. Therefore, time must be made to stand still, if necessary by the magic means of catatonic immobility—or by death. These are the extremes which are manifest in few, and latent in many cases of identity diffusion; yet, every adolescent, I would believe, knows at least fleeting moments of being at odds with time itself. In its normal and transitory form, this new kind of mistrust quickly or gradually yields to outlooks permitting and demanding an intense investment in a future, or in a number of possible futures. If these, to us, seem often quite "utopian" (i.e., based on expectations which would call for a change in the laws of historical change as we know them), we must, for the moment, postpone any judgment of value. The adolescent—or some adolescents—may need, at all costs, an outlook with a perspective worth an investment of energy. The actual realizability of such an outlook may be a matter of later learning and adjusting, and often a matter of historical luck.

In the following, I shall let each step on the chart lead to a few suggestive *social considerations* which were only briefly touched on in the foregoing. To envisage a future, the young adult may also need that something which Shaw called "a religion" and "a clear comprehension of life in the light of an intelligible theory." I indicated at the beginning that we would call this something-between-a-theory-and-a-religion an *ideology*, a term highly conducive to misunderstanding. At this point let me stress only the *temporal* element in world views which might be called ideological: they are grouped around *a utopian simplification of historical perspective* (salvation, conquest, reform, happiness, rationality, technological mastery) in accordance with newly developing identity potentials. Whatever else ideology is (Mannheim, 1949; Schilder 1930–1940), and whatever transitory or lasting social forms it takes, we will tentatively view it here and discuss it later—*as a necessity for the growing ego* which is involved in the succession of generations, and in adolescence is committed to some new synthesis of past and future: a synthesis which must include but transcend the past, even as identity does.

We proceed to *Identity Consciousness* (V, 2) the ancestors of which are *Doubt* and *Shame* (II, 2). They counteract and complicate the sense of autonomy, i.e., the acceptance of the psychosocial fact of being, once and for all, a separate individual, who actually and figuratively must stand on his own feet. Here, I beg to quote myself (1950a): "Shame is an emotion insufficiently studied,[13] because in our civilization it is so early and easily absorbed by guilt. Shame supposes that one is completely exposed and conscious of being looked at: in one word, self-conscious. One is visible and not ready to be visible; which is why we dream of shame as a situation in which we are stared at in a condition of incomplete dress. Shame is early expressed in an impulse to bury one's face, or to sink, right then and there, into the ground. But this, I think, is essentially rage turned against the self. He who is ashamed would like to force the world not to look at him, not to notice his exposure. He would like to destroy the eyes of the world. Instead he must wish for his own invisibility. . . . Doubt is the brother of shame. Where shame is dependent on the consciousness of being upright and exposed, doubt, so clinical observation leads me to believe, has much to do with a consciousness of having a front and a back—and especially a 'behind'. . . . This basic sense of doubt in whatever one has left behind forms a substratum for later and more verbal forms of compulsive doubting; which finds its adult expression in paranoiac fears concerning hidden persecutors and secret persecutions threatening from behind and from within the behind" (p. 223). Identity consciousness then is a new edition of that original *doubt*, which concerned the trustworthiness of the training adults and the trustworthiness of the child himself—only that in adolescence, such self-conscious doubt concerns the reliability and reconcilability of the whole span of childhood which is now to be left behind. The obligation now to achieve an identity, not only distinct but also distinctive, is apt to arouse a painful over-all *ashamedness*, somehow comparable to the original shame (and rage) over being visible all around to all-knowing adults—only that such potential shame now adheres to one's identity as a being with a *public history*, exposed to *age-mates* and *leaders*. All of this, in the normal course of events, is outbalanced by that *Self-certainty*, which comes from the accrued sense of an ever-increased identity at the conclusion of each previous crisis, a certainty now characterized by an increasing sense of independence from the family as the matrix of childhood identifications.

Among the societal phenomena corresponding to this second conflict there is a universal trend toward some form of *uniformity* (and sometimes to special uniforms or distinctive clothing) through which incomplete self-certainty, for a time, can hide in a group certainty, such as is provided by the badges as well as the sacrifices of investitures, confirmations, and initiations. Even those who care to differ radically must evolve a certain uniformity of differing (snobs, zoot-suiters). These and less obvious uniformities are supported by the institution of comprehensive *shaming* among peers, a judgmental give-and-take and free banding together which leaves only a few "holding the bag" in painful (if sometimes creative) isolation.

The matter of the choice of a *Negative Identity* (V, 3) as against free *Role Experimentation* has been discussed. The position of these terms on the chart signifies their obvious connection with the earlier conflict (III, 3) between free *Initiative* (in reality, fantasy, and play) and oedipal guilt. Where the identity crisis breaks through to the oedipal crisis and beyond it, to a crisis of trust, the choice of a negative identity remains the only form of initiative, complete denial of guilt or complete denial of ambition the only possible ways of managing guilt. On the other hand, the normal expression of relatively guilt-free initiative at this stage is a kind of disciplined role experimentation which follows the unwritten codes of adolescent subsocieties.

Of the social institutions which undertake to channel as they encourage such initiative, and to provide atonement as they appease guilt, we may point here, again, to *initiations* and *confirmations:* they strive, within an atmosphere of mythical timelessness, to combine some form of sacrifice or submission with an energetic guidance toward sanctioned and circumscribed ways of action—a combination which assures the development in the novice of an optimum of compliance with a maximum sense of fellowship and free choice. This ego aspect of the matter (namely, the achievement of a sense of a choice as a result of ritual regimentation) still awaits study and integration with the better explored sexual aspects of initiation rites and related rituals, official or spontaneous. Armies, of course, utilize this potentiality.

As we approach the middle region of the chart, we find that a more detailed discussion of the terms used has already been offered. Extreme *Work Paralysis* (V, 4) is the logical sequence of a deep sense of inadequacy (regressed to a sense of basic mistrust) of one's general equipment. Such a sense of inadequacy, of course, does not usually reflect a true lack of potential: it may rather convey the unrealistic demands made by an ego ideal willing to settle only for omnipotence or omniscience; it may express the fact that the immediate social environment does not have a niche for the individual's true gifts; or it may reflect the paradoxical fact that an individual in early school life was seduced into a specialized precocity which early outdistanced his identity development. All of these reasons, then, may exclude the individual from that experimental competition in play and work through which he learns to find and to insist on *his* kind of achievement and work identity.

Social institutions support the strength and the distinctiveness of work identity by offering those who are still learning and experimenting a certain *status-of-the-moratorium*, an apprenticeship or discipleship characterized by defined duties, sanctioned competitions, and special freedoms, and yet potentially integrated with the hierarchies of expectable jobs and careers, castes and classes, guilds and unions.

In box V, 5 we again meet the diagonal, and the over-all focus of this paper; crossing it we enter the area of psychosocial elements which are not derivatives but precursors of future psychosocial crises. The first such element (V, 6) is *Sexual Identity vs. Bisexual Diffusion*, the most immediate precursor of *Intimacy vs. Isolation*. Here the sexual mores of cultures and classes make for immense differences in the psychosocial differentiation of masculine and feminine (M. Mead, 1949), and in the age, kind, and ubiquity of genital activity. These differences can obscure the common fact discussed above, namely, that the development of psychosocial intimacy is not possible without a firm sense of identity. Bisexual diffusion can lead young adults toward two deceptive developments. Induced by special mores, or otherwise seduced, they may foreclose their identity development by concentrating on early genital activity without intimacy; or, on the contrary, they may concentrate on social or intellectual status values which underplay the genital element, with a resulting permanent weakness of genital polarization with the other sex. Different mores (Kinsey, Pomeroy, and Martin, 1948) demand from some the ability to postpone genital activity, and from others, the early ability to make it a "natural" part of life: in some cases, special problems ensue which may well impair true heterosexual intimacy in young adulthood.

Social institutions here offer ideological rationales for a *prolongation of the psychosexual moratorium* in the form of complete sexual abstinence, in the form of genital activity without social commitment, or in the form of sexual play without genital engagement (petting). What a group's or an individual's "libido economy" will stand for depends to some extent on the identity gain which accrues from such preferred sexual behavior.

The study of horizontal V of the chart, then, reveals certain systematic consistencies in the described elements of identity diffusion, and in those of identity formation. As pointed out parenthetically, these consistencies correspond to certain social institutions, which (in ways still to be elucidated) support the ego needs and ego functions subsumed under the term "identity." In fact, the two remaining boxes of horizontal V (which at any rate are marginal to this clinical section) cannot be approached at all without a discussion of social institutions. The prime institution which awaits clarification here is that system of ideals which societies present to the young individual in the explicit or implicit form of an *ideology*. To ideology we may, in tentative summary, ascribe the function of offering youth (1) an overly clear perspective of the future, encompassing all foreseeable time, and thus counteracting individual "time diffusion"; (2) an opportunity for the exhibition of some uniformity of appearance and action counteracting individual identity consciousness; (3) inducement to collective role and work experimentation which can counteract a sense of inhibition and personal guilt; (4) submission to leaders who as "big brothers" escape the ambivalence of the parent-child relation; (5) introduction into the ethos of the prevailing technology, and thus into sanctioned and regulated competition; and (6) a seeming correspondence between the internal world of ideals and evils, on the one hand, and, on the other, the outer world with its organized goals and dangers in real space and time: a geographic-historical framework for the young individual's budding identity.

I am aware of having, in the conclusion of pathographic sketch, "sketched in" some references to phenomena which are the domain of social science. I can justify this only with the assumption that clinical work, in cutting through the immense diversity of individual pathology in order to arrive at some workable generalities, may well come upon an aspect of matters institutional which the historical and the economic approach has necessarily neglected. Here, however, we must first attempt to bring some order into the terminological household of our own field, and this especially where it overlaps with areas of social science.

SOCIETAL: EGO AND ENVIRONMENT

1

It has not escaped the reader that the term "identity" covers much of what has been called the "self" by a variety of workers, be it in the form of a self-concept (George H. Mead, 1934), a self-system (Harry S. Sullivan, 1946–1947), or in that of fluctuating self-experiences described by Schilder (1934), Federn (1927–1949), and others.[14] Within psychoanalytic ego psychology, Hartmann, above all, has circumscribed this general area more clearly when in discussing the so-called *libidinal cathexis of the ego in narcissism*, he comes to the conclusion that it is rather a self which is thus being cathected. He advocates a term *"self-representation,"* as differentiated from "object representation" (Hartmann, 1950). This self-representation was, less systematically, anticipated by Freud in his occasional references to the ego's "attitudes toward the self" and to fluctuating cathexes bestowed upon this self in labile states of "self-esteem" (Freud, 1914). In this paper, we are concerned with the *genetic continuity* of such a self-representation—a continuity which must lastly be ascribed to the work of the ego. No other inner agency could accomplish the selective accentuation of significant identifications throughout childhood and the gradual integration of self-images in anticipation of an identity. It is for this reason that I have called identity, at first, ego identity. But in brashly choosing a name analogous to "ego ideal," I have opened myself to the query as to what the relationship of these two concepts is.

Freud assigned the *internalized perpetuation* of cultural influences to the functions of the "superego or ego ideal" which was to represent the commands and the prohibitions emanating from the environment and its traditions. Let us compare two statements of Freud's which are relevant here. ". . . the super-ego of the child is not really built up on the model of the parents, but on that of the parents' super-ego; it takes over the same content, it becomes the vehicle of tradition and of all the age-long values which have been handed down in this way from generation to generation. You may easily guess what great help is afforded by the recognition of the super-ego in understanding the social behavior of man, in grasping the problem of delinquency, for example, and perhaps, too, in providing us with some practical hints upon education. . . . Mankind never lives completely in the present; the *ideologies of the super-ego*[15] perpetuate the past, the traditions of the race and the people, which yield but slowly to the influence of the present and to new developments, and, so long as they work through the super-ego, play an important part in man's life" (Freud, 1932, pp. 95–96). Freud, it is to be noted here, speaks of the "ideologies of the super-ego," thus giving the superego ideational content; yet he also refers to it as a "vehicle," i.e., as a part of the psychic system through which ideas work. It would seem that by ideologies of the superego Freud means the superego's specific contributions to the archaic, to the magic in the inner coerciveness of ideologies.

In a second statement Freud acknowledges the social side of the ego ideal. "The ego ideal opens up an important avenue for the understanding of group psychology. In addition to its individual side, this ideal has a social side; it is also the common ideal of a family, a class or a nation" (Freud, 1914, p. 101).

It would seem that the terms "superego" and "ego ideal" have come to be distinguished by their different relation to phylogenetic and to ontogenetic history. The superego is conceived as a more archaic and thoroughly internalized representative of the evolutionary principle of morality, of man's *congenital proclivity* toward the development of a primitive, categorical conscience. Allied with (ontogenetically) early introjects, the superego remains a rigidly vindictive and punitive inner agency of "blind" morality. The ego ideal, however, seems to be more flexibly bound to the ideals of the particular *historical period* and thus is closer to the ego function of reality testing.

Ego identity (if we were to hold on to this term and to this level of discourse) would in comparison be even closer to *social reality* in that as a subsystem of the ego it would test, select, and integrate the self-representations derived from the psychosocial crises of childhood. It could be said to be characterized by the more or less *actually attained but forever-to-be-revised* sense of the reality of the self within social reality; while the imagery of the ego ideal could be said to represent a set of *to-be-strived-for but forever-not-quite-attainable ideal* goals for the self.

However, in using the word "self" in the sense of Hartmann's self-representation, one opens the whole controversy to a radical consideration. One could argue that it may be wise in matters of the ego's perceptive and regulative dealings with its self to reserve the designation "ego" for the subject, and to give the designation "self" to the object. The ego, then, as a central organizing agency, is during the course of life faced with a changing self which, in turn, demands to be synthesized with abandoned and anticipated selves. This suggestion would be applicable to the *body ego*, which could be said to be the part of the self provided by the attributes of the organism, and, therefore, might more appropriately be called the *body self;* it would also concern the ego ideal as the representative of the ideas, images, and configurations which serve the persistent comparison with an *ideal self*; and finally, it would apply to what I have called *ego identity*. What could consequently be called the *self-identity* emerges from all those experiences in which a sense of temporary self-diffusion was successfully contained by a renewed and ever more realistic self-definition and social recognition. *Identity formation thus can be said to have a self-aspect, and an ego aspect.* It is part of the ego in the sense that it represents the ego's synthesizing function on one of its frontiers, namely, the actual social structure of the environment and the image of reality as transmitted to the child during successive childhood crises. (The other frontiers would be the id, and the demands made on the ego by our biological history and structure; the superego and the demands of our more primitively moralistic proclivities; and the ego ideal with its idealized parent images.) Identity, in this connection, has a claim to recognition as the adolescent ego's most important support, in the task of containing the postpubertal id, and in balancing the then newly invoked superego as well as the again overly demanding ego ideal.

Until the matter of ego versus self is sufficiently defined to permit a terminological decision, I shall use the bare term "identity" in order to suggest a social function of the ego which results, in adolescence, in a relative psychosocial equilibrium essential to the tasks of young adulthood.

2

The word "psychosocial" so far has had to serve as an emergency bridge between the so-called "biological" formulations of psychoanalysis and newer ones which take the cultural environment into more systematic consideration.

The so-called basic *biological* orientation of psychoanalysis has gradually become a habitual kind of *pseudo biology*, and this especially in the conceptualization (or lack thereof) of man's "environment." In psychoanalytic writings the terms "outer world" or "environment" are often used to designate an uncharted area which is said to be outside merely because it fails to be inside—inside the individual's somatic skin, or inside his psychic systems, or inside his self in the widest sense. Such a vague and yet omnipresent "outerness" by necessity assumes a number of ideological connotations, and, in fact, assumes the character of a number of world images: sometimes "the outer world" is conceived of as reality's conspiracy against the infantile wish world; sometimes as the (indifferent or annoying) fact of the existence of other people; and then again as the (at least partially benevolent) presence of maternal care. But even in the recent admission of the significance of the "mother-child relationship," a stubborn tendency persists to treat the mother-child unit as a "biological" entity more or less isolated from its cultural surroundings, which then again become an "environment" of vague supports or of blind pressures and mere "conventions." Thus, step for step, we are encumbered by the remnants of juxtapositions which were once necessary and fruitful enough: for it was important to establish the fact that moralistic and hypocritical social demands are apt to crush the adult and to exploit the child. It was important to conceptualize certain intrinsic antagonisms between the individual's and society's energy households. However, the implicit conclusion that an individual ego could exist against or without a specifically human "environment," i.e., social organization, is senseless; and, far from being "biological" in its orientation, threatens to isolate psychoanalytic theory from the rich ethological and ecological findings of modern biology.

It is again Hartmann (1939) who opens the way to new considerations. His statement that the human infant is born preadapted to an "average expectable environment" implies a more truly biological as well as an inescapably societal formulation. For not even the very best of mother-child relationships could, by themselves, account for that subtle and complex "milieu" which permits a human baby not only to survive but also to develop his potentialities for growth and uniqueness. Man's ecology includes among its dimensions constant natural, historical, and technological readjustment; which makes it at once obvious that only a perpetual social metabolism and a constant (if ever so imperceptible) restructuring of tradition can safeguard for each new generation of infants anything approaching an "average expectability" of environment. Today, when rapid technological changes have taken the lead, the matter of establishing by scientific means and of preserving in flexible forms an "average expectable" continuity in child rearing and education has, in fact, become a matter of human survival.

The specific kind of preadaptedness of the human infant (namely, the readiness to grow by predetermined steps through institutionalized psychosocial crises) calls not only for one basic environment, but for a whole chain of such successive environments. As the child "adapts" in spurts and stages, he has a claim, at any given stage reached, to the next "average expectable environment." In other words, the human environment must permit and safeguard a series of more or less discontinuous and yet culturally and psychologically consistent steps, each extending further along the radius of expanding life tasks. All of this makes man's so-called biological adaptation a matter of life cycles developing within their community's changing history. Consequently, a psychoanalytic sociology faces the task of conceptualizing man's environment as the persistent endeavor of the older and more adult egos to join in the organizational effort of providing an integrated series of average expectable environments for the young egos.

3

In a recent paper which thoughtfully yet somewhat sweepingly reviews efforts at approaching the relation of culture and personality, Hartmann, Kris, and Loewenstein (1951) state: "Cultural conditions could and should be viewed also with the question in mind which and what kind of opportunities for ego functions in a sphere free from conflict they invite or inhibit." In regard to the possibility of studying the reflection of such "cultural conditions" in the psychoanalysis of individuals, the writers seems less encouraging. They state: "Analysts too are aware of differences of behavior caused by cultural conditions; they are not devoid of that common sense which has always stressed these differences, but their impact on the analytic observer tends to decrease as work progresses and as available data move from the periphery to the center, that is from manifest behavior to data, part of which is accessible only to an analytic investigation." The present paper ventures to suggest that rather central problems of ego development, which are, indeed, "accessible only to an analytic investigation," demand that the psychoanalyst's awareness of cultural differences go well beyond that "common sense" which the three authors (being themselves outstanding cosmopolitans) seem to find sufficient in this particular area of observation, while they would assuredly urge a more "analyzed" common sense in other areas.

In order to approach this whole matter psychoanalytically, it may well be necessary for the individual psychoanalyst to ask himself what particular configuration of drives, defenses, capabilities, and opportunities led him into the choice of this ever-expanding field. Some search in this area may clarify the fact that some of the most heated and stubborn answers to the question of what psychoanalysis *is* or *is not* originate in another question of great urgency, namely: what psychoanalysis *must be* (or *must remain or become*) to a particular worker because a particular psychoanalytic "identity" has become a cornerstone of his existence as a man, a professional, and a citizen. I am not denying here the necessity, in a suddenly expanding and unexpectedly popular field, to define the original sources of its inspiration and the fundamentals of its specific morality. Yet, psychoanalysis, in its young history, has offered rich opportunities for a variety of identities: it gave new function and scope to such divergent endeavors as natural philosophy and Talmudic argument; medical tradition and missionary teaching; literary demonstration and the building of theory; social reform and the making of money.

Psychoanalysis as a movement has harbored a variety of world images and utopias which originated in the various stages of its history in a variety of countries, and this is a result of the simple fact that man, in order to be able to interact efficiently with other human beings, must, at intervals, make *a total orientation out of a given stage of partial knowledge.* Individual students of Freud thus found their identity best suited to certain early theses of his which promised a particular sense of psychoanalytic identity, and with it, an inspiring ideology. Similarly, overstated antitheses to some of Freud's tentative and transient theses have served as bases for professional and scientific identities of other workers in the field. Such identities easily find elaboration in ideological schools and in irreversible systematizations which do not permit of argument or change.

In speaking of scientific proof and scientific progress in a field which deals directly with the immediate needs of men, it is necessary to account not only for methodological, practical, and ethical factors, but also for the necessity of a professional identity backed by an ideological quasi synthesis of the available orientations. Sooner or later, then, training analyses must encompass the varieties of professional identity formation in candidates-for-training, while theoretical teaching must throw light also on the ideological background of principal differences in what is felt to be most practical, most true, and most right at various stages of this developing field.

<h3 style="text-align:center">4</h3>

The discussion of "professional identities" has necessarily led us beyond identity formation proper, to its derivatives in later, truly adult stages. I will make one more step into adulthood, before returning, in conclusion, to the problem of ideological polarization as an aspect of the societal processes which meets a necessity of adolescent ego development.

I have already implied a hypothesis which goes beyond that of Hartmann, Kris, and Loewenstein (1951), who state that "cultural conditions could and should be viewed *also*[16] with the question in mind which and what kind of opportunities for ego functions in a sphere free from conflict they invite or inhibit." It may well be that the relationship between the organized values and institutional efforts of societies, on the one hand, and the mechanisms of ego synthesis, on the other, is more systematic; and that, from a psychosocial point of view at any rate, basic social and cultural processes can *only* be viewed as the joint endeavor of adult egos to develop and maintain, through joint organization, a maximum of conflict-free energy in a mutually supportive psychosocial equilibrium. Only such organization is likely to give consistent support to the young egos at every step of their development.

I have characterized the psychosocial gains of adult ego development with the terms *Intimacy*, *Generativity*, and *Integrity* (VI, 6; VII, 7; VIII, 8 on the chart). They denote a postadolescent development of libidinal cathexes in *intimate engagements;* in parenthood or other *forms of "generating"*;[17] and, finally, in the most *integrative experiences* and values accrued from a lifetime. All of these developments have ego aspects and social aspects; in fact, their very alternatives, *Isolation* (VI, 6), *Self-absorption* (VII, 7), and *Despair* (VIII, 8), can be held in check only by the individual's fitting participation in social endeavors which "invite opportunities for ego functions in spheres free from conflict." The older generation thus needs the younger one as much as the younger one depends on the older; and it would seem that it is in this mutuality of the development of the older and younger generations that certain basic and universal values such as love, faith, truth, justice, order, work, etc., in all of their defensive strength, compensatory power, and independent creativity become and remain important joint achievements of individual ego development and of the social process. In fact, as our clinical histories begin to reveal, these values provide indispensable support for the ego development of the growing generations, in that they give some specific superindividual consistency to parental conduct (although *kinds* of consistency—including consistent kinds of being inconsistent—vary with value systems and personality types).

The intrinsic complication and the peculiar social pathology adhering to the *verbal conventions* and *formal institutions* which communicate and perpetuate social values periodically call for special societal processes which will recreate the "average expectability" of the environments either through ceremonial rededication, or through systematic reformulation. In both cases, selected leaders and elites feel called upon to demonstrate a convincing, a "charismatic" kind of generalized generativity, i.e., a superpersonal interest in the maintenance and the rejuvenation of institutions. In recorded history, some such leaders are registered as "great"; they, it seems, are able, out of the deepest personal conflicts to derive the energy which meets their period's specific needfulness for a resynthesis of the prevalent world image. At any rate, only through constant rededication will institutions gain the active and inspired investment of new energy from their young members. More theoretically stated: only by maintaining, in its institutionalized values, meaningful correspondences to the main crises of ego development, does a society manage to have at the disposal of its particular group identity a maximum of the conflict-free energy accrued from the childhood crises of a majority of its young members.[18]

Before briefly applying this general assumption to ideology, I must ask the reader to take one more look at the chart. In boxes V, 6; V, 7; and V, 8 he will find whatever indication I can give of the precursors in adolescence of what later on are *Intimacy, Generativity,* and *Integrity*. The struggle for *Sexual Identity* (V, 6), while, at first, consumed with the question as to what kind of a male or female one is, through the selective search for *Intimacy* (VI, 6), approaches the problem of a choice of a future co-parent. The clarification, through a firmer identity formation, of one's status as a *follower* (of some) and a *leader* (of others) (V, 7), permits the early development of a responsibility toward younger age-mates which, although an important social phenomenon in its own right, is a precursor of the sense of responsibility for the next generation *(Generativity,* VII, 7). Finally, some form of *Ideological Polarization* (V, 8), some breakdown of the multiplicity of values into a few which coerce commitment, must be part and parcel of this gradual reversal of roles, through which the "identified" individual becomes a figure of identification for the young. Such polarization, however, cannot fail eventually to become a critical part of the problem of *Integrity* (VIII, 8), a matter which we saw reflected in Shaw's statement (1952) that he "succeeded only too well" in living the public identity "G. B. S.," i.e., in the polarization of his propensities for acting like an actor on the stage of life, and for acting as a reformer in social reality.

5

Shaw, of course, was a studiedly spectacular man. But, to extend a Shavianism quoted above: a clown is often not only the best but also the most sincere part of the Great Show. It is, therefore, worth while at this point to review the words chosen by Shaw to characterize the story of his "conversion": "I was *drawn into* the Socialist *revival* of the early eighties, among Englishmen *intensely serious* and *burning with indignation* at very *real* and very *fundamental evils* that affected *all the world.*" The words here italicized convey to me the following implications. "Drawn into": an ideology has a compelling power. "Revival": it consists of a traditional force in the state of rejuvenation. "Intensely serious": it permits even the cynical to make an investment of sincerity. "Burning with indignation": it gives to the need for repudiation the sanction of righteousness. "Real": it projects a vague inner evil onto a circumscribed horror in reality. "Fundamental": it promises participation in an effort at basic reconstruction of society. "All the world": it gives structure to a totally defined world image. Here, then, are the elements by which a group identity harnesses in the service of its ideology the young individual's aggressive and discriminative energies, and encompasses, as it completes it, the individual's identity. Thus, identity and ideology are two aspects of the same process. Both provide the necessary condition for further individual maturation and, with it, for the next higher form of identification, namely, the *solidarity linking common iden-*

tities. For the need to bind irrational self-hate and irrational repudiation makes young people, on occasion, mortally compulsive and conservative even where and when they seem most anarchic and radical; the same need makes them potentially "ideological," i.e., more or less explicitly in search of a world image held together by what Shaw called "a clear comprehension of life in the light of an intelligible theory."

As far as Fabian Socialists are concerned, Shaw seems fully justified in using terms characterizing an ideology of marked intellectual brilliance. More generally, an ideological system is a coherent body of shared images, ideas, and ideals which (whether based on a formulated dogma, an implicit *Weltanschauung*, a highly structured world image, a political creed, or a "way of life") provides for the participants a coherent, if systematically simplified, over-all orientation in space and time, in means and ends.

The word "ideology" itself has somewhat of a bad name. By their very nature ideologies contradict other ideologies as "inconsistent" and hypocritical; and an over-all critique of ideology characterizes its persuasive simplifications as a systematic form of collective hypocrisy (Mannheim, 1949). For it is true that the average adult, and in fact, the average community, if not acutely engaged in some ideological polarization, are apt to consign ideology to a well-circumscribed compartment in their lives, where it remains handy for periodical rituals and rationalizations, but will do no undue harm to other business at hand. Yet, the fact that ideologies are simplified conceptions of what is to come (and thus later can serve as rationalizations for what has come about) does not preclude the possibility that at certain stages of individual development and at certain periods in history, ideological polarization, conflict, and commitment correspond to an inescapable inner need. Youth needs to base its rejections and acceptances on ideological alternatives vitally related to the existing range of alternatives for identity formation.

Ideologies seem to provide meaningful combinations of the

oldest and the newest in a group's ideals. They thus channel the forceful earnestness, the sincere asceticism, and the eager indignation of youth toward that social frontier where the struggle between conservatism and radicalism is most alive. On that frontier, fanatic ideologists do their busy work and psychopathic leaders their dirty work; but there, also, true leaders create significant solidarities. All ideologies ask for, as the prize for the promised possession of a future, uncompromising commitment to some absolute hierarchy of values and some rigid principle of conduct: be that principle total obedience to tradition, if the future is the eternalization of ancestry; total resignation, if the future is to be of another world; total martial discipline, if the future is to be reserved for some brand of armed superman; total inner reform, if the future is perceived as an advanced edition of heaven on earth; or (to mention only one of the ideological ingredients of our time) complete pragmatic abandon to the processes of production and to human teamwork, if unceasing production seems to be the thread which holds present and future together. It is in the totalism and exclusiveness of some ideologies that the superego is apt to regain its territory from identity: for when established identities become outworn or unfinished ones threaten to remain incomplete, special crises compel men to wage holy wars, by the cruelest means, against those who seem to question or threaten their unsafe ideological bases.

We may well pause to ponder briefly the fact that the technological and economic developments of our day encroach upon all traditional group identities and solidarities such as may have developed in agrarian, feudal, patrician, or mercantile ideologies. As has been shown by many writers, such over-all development seems to result in a loss of a sense of cosmic wholeness, of providential planfulness, and of heavenly sanction for the means of production (and destruction). In large parts of the world, this seems to result in a ready fascination with totalistic world views, views predicting milleniums and cataclysms, and advocating self-appointed mortal gods. Technological centralization

today can give small groups of such fanatic ideologists the concrete power of totalitarian state machines (Erikson, 1953).

Psychoanalysis has made some contributions to the understanding of these developments, especially in so far as they reflect
the universal anxieties, inner dependencies, and vulnerabilities
adhering to the common fact of human childhood. Psychoanalysis
can also help to understand the fact that even in civilized beings
the superego's paternalistic-primitive simplicity may call for an
irrational trust in superpolice chiefs on earth, now that the
heavenly discipline which encompassed earlier world images
seems to have lost its convincing firmness. However, the application of the psychoanalytic instrument to the questions as to how
man changes in his depth as he changes the expanses of his
environment, and as to who is affected (and how, and how deeply)
by technological and ideological changes (Erikson, 1953)—these
questions must await better formulations of the ego's relationship
to work techniques, to the technological "environment," and to
the prevalent division of labor.

6

In a recent seminar in Jerusalem[19] I had an opportunity to
discuss with Israeli scholars and clinicians the question of what
the identity of an "Israeli" is, and thus to envisage one extreme of
contemporary ideological orientations. Israel fascinates both her
friends and her enemies. A great number of ideological fragments
from European history have found their way into the consciousness of this small state; and many of the identity problems which
have occupied a century and a half of American history are being
faced in Israel within a few years. A new nation is established on a
distant coast (which does not seem to "belong" to anybody) out of
oppressed minorities from many lands, a new identity based on
imported ideals which are libertarian, puritanic, and messianic.
Any discussion of Israel's manifold and most immediate problems
sooner or later leads to the extraordinary accomplishments and
the extraordinary ideological problems posed by the pioneer

Zionist settlers (now a small minority) who make up what is
known as the Kibbutz movement. These European ideologists,
given—as it were—a *historical moratorium* created by the peculiar
international and national status of Palestine first in the Ottoman
Empire and then in the British mandate, were able to establish
and to fortify a significant *utopian bridgehead* for Zionist ideology.
In his "homeland," and tilling his very home soil, the "ingathered"
Jew was to overcome such evil identities as result from eternal
wandering, merchandising, and intellectualizing (Erikson, 1950a)
and was to become *whole* again in body and mind, as well as in
nationality. That the Kibbutz movement has created a hardy,
responsible, and inspired type of individual, nobody could deny,
although certain details of its educational system (such as the
raising of children, from the very beginning, in Children's Houses,
and the rooming together of boys and girls through the high-
school years) are under critical scrutiny, both in Israel and abroad.
The fact is, however, that in Israel a utopia was established on a
frontier exposed all around, under conditions reminiscent of those
faced by the Mormons. This historical fact is the only framework
for judging the rationale and the rationalizations of the style of life
which ensued. For no doubt, these pioneers (comparable to this
country's settlers, who, in turn, utilized the historical moratorium
offered by the discovery of an empty continent, for the establishment of a new "way of life") provided a new nation, sprung up
overnight, with a historical ideal. A legitimate question, however,
and one not too foreign to this country's historians, concerns the
relationship of a revolutionary elite to those who subsequently
crowd into and thrive on the lands occupied and on the gains
made.[20] In Israel, the by now somewhat exclusive elite of Kib-
butzniks faces that incomparably larger part of the population
which represents an ideologically all but indigestible mixture: the
masses of African and Oriental immigrants, powerful organized
labor, the big city dwellers, the religious orthodoxy, the new state
bureaucracy—and then, of course, the "good old" mercantile class
of middlemen. Furthermore, the more uncompromising part of

the Kibbutz movement has not failed to place itself between the two worlds to both of which Zionism maintains strong historical bonds: American and British Jewry (which bought much of the Kibbutz land from Arab absentee landlords) and Soviet Communism, to which the (shall we say) communalistic Kibbutz movement[21] felt ideologically close—only to be repudiated by Moscow as another form of deviationism.

The Kibbutz movement thus is one example of a modern ideological utopia which freed unknown energies in young people who considered themselves as of one "people," and created a (more or less explicit) group ideal of pervading significance—if of quite unpredictable historical fate in an industrial world. However, Israel is, undoubtedly, one of the most ideology-conscious countries that ever existed; no "peasants" nor workmen ever argued more about the far-reaching meanings of daily decisions. The subtler meanings of ideology for identity formation can probably be fathomed best by comparing highly verbal ideologies with those transitory systems of conversion and aversion which exist in any society, in that no-man's land between childhood and adulthood more or less derisively called adolescence—exist as the most meaningful part of a young person's or a young group's life, often without the knowledge, or indeed, curiosity, of the adults around them. It must be assumed that much of the spontaneous polarization of tastes, opinions, and slogans which occupy the arguments of young people, and much of the sudden impulse to join in destructive behavior, are loose ends of identity formation waiting to be tied together by some ideology.

7

In the pathographic section of this paper I have pointed to the *total choice* of a negative identity in individuals who could achieve such escape on the basis of autistic and regressive proclivities.

The escape of many gifted if unstable young individuals into a private utopia or, as another patient put it, a "majority of one," might not be necessary were it not for a general development to which they feel unable to submit, i.e., the increasing demand for standardization, uniformity, and conformity which characterizes the present stage of this our individualist civilization. In this country, the demand for large-scale conformity has not developed into an explicit totalitarian ideology; it has associated itself with the total dogmas of churches and with the stereotypes of businesslike behavior, but, on the whole, shuns political ideology. We appreciate, as we study it, the capacity of our youth to manage the identity diffusion of an industrial democracy with simple trustfulness, with playful dissonance, with technical virtuosity, with "other-minded" solidarity (Riesman, 1950)—and with a distaste for ideological explicitness. What exactly the implicit ideology of American youth (this most technological youth in the world) is—that is a fateful question, not to be lightly approached in a paper of this kind. Nor would one dare to assess in passing the changes which may be taking place in this ideology and in its implicitness, as a result of a world struggle which makes a military identity a necessary part of young adulthood in this country.

It is easier to delineate that malignant turn toward a *negative group identity* which prevails in some of the youth especially of our large cities, where conditions of economic, ethnic, and religious marginality provide poor bases for positive identities: here negative group identities are sought in spontaneous clique formations ranging all the way from neighborhood gangs and jazz mobs, to dope rings, homosexual circles, and criminal gangs. Clinical experience can be expected to make significant contributions to this problem.[22] Yet, we may well warn ourselves against an uncritical transfer of clinical terms, attitudes, and methods to such public problems. Rather we may come back to a point made earlier: teachers, judges, and psychiatrists, who deal with youth, come to be significant representatives of that strategic act of "recognition" (the act through which society "identifies" its young members and thus contributes to their developing identity) which was described at the beginning of this paper. If, for simplicity's sake or in order to accommodate ingrown habits of law or psychiatry, they diagnose and treat as a criminal, as a constitutional misfit, as a derelict doomed by his upbringing, or—indeed—as a deranged patient, a young person who, for reasons of personal or social marginality, is close to choosing a negative identity, that young person may well put his energy into becoming exactly what the careless and fearful community expects him to be—and make a total job of it.

It is hoped that the theory of identity, in the long run, can contribute more to this problem than to sound a warning.

SUMMARY

In my attempt to circumscribe the problem of identity I have been "all over the map." I do not propose to leave the matter in this condition: as far as is possible, studies taking into account the specific dynamic nature of selected media (life history, case history, dream life, ideology) will follow (Erikson, 1958a). In the meantime, and in summary: identity, in outbalancing at the conclusion of childhood the potentially malignant dominance of the infantile superego, permits the individual to forgo excessive self-repudiation and the diffused repudiation of otherness. Such freedom provides a necessary condition for the ego's power to integrate matured sexuality, ripened capacities, and adult commitments. The histories of our young patients illustrate the ways in which aggravated identity crises may result from special genetic causes and from specific dynamic conditions. Such studies, in turn, throw new light on those more or less institutionalized rites and rituals, associations, and movements, through which societies and subsocieties grant youth a world between childhood and adulthood: a psychosocial moratorium during which extremes of *subjective experience*, alternatives of *ideological choice*, and potentialities of *realistic commitment* can become the subject of social play and of joint mastery.

Appendix: Worksheet

THIS WORKSHEET summarizes in diagrammatic form the areas and stages of development discussed in this monograph. Being a worksheet it has undergone and will undergo both changes and expansion; being a diagram it flatly separates groupings and sequences which, under observation, prove to be overlapping. Nevertheless, it is suggested that both verticals and horizontals represent a kind of skeleton essential to whatever flesh and blood may (and must) be added by study and discussion. Such study can be enhanced by arranging each vertical along a diagonal (as in the epigenetic chart, p. 129), and by observing its inner consistency before relating it to other columns. There is no rank order; one can begin with any column for which the available data are plentiful and proceed to the next promising column.

Worksheet

	A Psychosocial Crises	B Radius of Significant Relations	C Related Elements of Social Order	D Psychosocial Modalities	E Psychosexual Stages
I	Trust vs. Mistrust	Maternal Person	Cosmic Order	To get / To give in return	Oral-Respiratory Sensory-Kinesthetic (Incorporative Modes)
II	Autonomy vs. Shame, Doubt	Parental Persons	"Law and Order"	To hold (on) / To let (go)	Anal-Urethral, Muscular (Retentive-Eliminative)
III	Initiative vs. Guilt	Basic Family	Ideal Prototypes	To make (=going after) / To "make like" (=playing)	Infantile-Genital, Locomotor (Intrusive, Inclusive)
IV	Industry vs. Inferiority	"Neighborhood," School	Technological Elements	To make things (=completing) / To make things together	"Latency"
V	Identity and Repudiation vs. Identity Diffusion	Peer Groups and Outgroups; Models of Leadership	Ideological Perspectives	To be oneself (or not to be) / To share being oneself	Puberty
VI	Intimacy and Solidarity vs. Isolation	Partners in Friendship Sex, Competition, Cooperation	Patterns of Cooperation and Competition	To lose and find oneself in another	Genitality
VII	Generativity vs. Self-absorption	Divided Labor and Shared Household	Currents of Education and Tradition	To make be / To take care of	
VIII	Integrity vs. Despair	"Mankind" "My Kind"	Wisdom	To be, through having been / To face not being	

Notes

1. Ego Development and Historical Change

1. A psychoanalyst with an outstanding historical orientation repeated even in 1944 that "each member of a large mass of people is an individual and a nonindividual, a particle of a mass subject to many psychological laws different from those under which he primarily functions when alone, at home" (Zilboorg, 1944, p. 6).

If, for the moment, we accept as representative the image of a man who is geographically completely alone (and this, of all places, at home), it is questionable that the psychological laws governing his aloneness are really different from those which guide him in a "mass." Would it not be more accurate to say: the situation differs—and with it the thresholds of consciousness and of motility, the available channels of communication and the available techniques of expression and action? That a man could ever be psychologically alone; that a man, "alone," is essentially "better" than the same man in a group; that a man in a temporary solitary condition has ceased to be a political animal, and has disengaged himself from social action (or inaction) on whatever class level; these and similar stereotypes deserve to be accepted only in order to be further analyzed.

2. In Fenichel's comprehensive volume of the theory of neurosis (1945) the subject of social prototypes is only introduced toward the end of the chapter on mental development, and then in the form of a negation: "Neither a belief in 'ideal models' nor a certain degree of 'social fear' is necessarily pathological." The problem of the superego's origin in society is not discussed until page 463, in the chapter on character disorders.

3. This paper is in sequence with "Childhood and Tradition in Two American Indian Tribes" (Erikson, 1945) and overlaps with it in this introductory part.

4. As explained in detail elsewhere (Erikson, 1945), such a collective fixation point is a meaningful part of the total instinctive self-regulation of a culture.

5. This has certain obvious implications for the "re-education" of "bad" nations. It can be predicted that no admission of having sinned and no promises to be good will make a nation "democratic" unless the new identity offered can be integrated with previous concepts of strong and weak, masculine and feminine, based on experiences in the geographic-historical matrix of the nation and in the childhood of the individual. Only a victor who demonstrates the historical inescapability of supernatural aims and knows how to base them on established regional identities will make new people out of old nations.

6. In an outstanding document, Bruno Bettelheim (1943) has described his experiences in a German concentration camp of the early days. He reports the various steps and

external manifestations (such as affectations in posture and dress) by which the inmates abandoned their identity as anti-Fascists in favor of that of their tormentors. He himself preserved his life and sanity by deliberately and persistently clinging to the historical Jewish identity of invincible spiritual and intellectual superiority over a physically superior outer world: he made his tormentors the subject of a silent research project which he safely delivered to the world of free letters.

7. In the inventory of our patients' ideal and evil prototypes we meet face to face the clinical facts on which Jung based his theory of inherited prototypes ("archetypes"). As for this theory, we may note in passing that the first conceptual controversies in psychoanalysis throw light on the problem of identity in the initial stages of a science. Jung, it seems, could find a sense of identity in psychoanalytic work only by a juxtaposition of his ancestors' mystical space-time and whatever he sensed in Freud's ancestry. His scientific rebellion thus led to ideological regression and (weakly denied) political reaction. This phenomenon—like similar ones before and after—had its group-psychological counterpart in reaction within the psychoanalytic movement: as if in fear of endangering a common group identity based on common scientific gains, psychoanalytic observers chose to ignore not only Jung's interpretations but the facts he observed.

Certain phenomena underlying such concepts as the "anima" and the "animus" (which I seem to recognize in my woman patient's erect image) play a dominant role in ego development. The synthesizing function of the ego constantly works on subsuming in fewer and fewer images and personified Gestalten the fragments and loose ends of all the infantile identifications. In doing so it not only uses existing historical prototypes; it also employs individually methods of condensation and of pictorial representation which characterize the products of collective imagery. In Jung's "persona" we see a weak ego sell out to a compelling social prototype. A fake ego identity is established which suppresses rather than synthesizes those experiences and functions which endanger the "front." A dominant prototype of masculinity, for example, forces a man to exclude from his ego identity all that which characterizes the evil image of the lesser sex, the castrate. This leaves much of his receptive and maternal faculties dissimulated, undeveloped, and guilt-ridden, and makes a shell of mannishness out of what is left.

8. According to a communication by Gordon McGregor, Sioux mixed-bloods on Pine Ridge Reservation call Sioux full-bloods "niggers," only to be called, in turn, "white trash."

9. Notable exceptions are the recipients of promising commissions and members of teams in highly mechanized units. However, men whose ego identity thrives on military service sometimes break down after discharge, when it appears that the war provoked them into the usurpation of more ambitious prototypes than their more restricted peacetime identities could afford to sustain.

10. This basic plan was established, among others, in Freud's publication "'Civilized' Sexual Morality and Modern Nervousness" (1908) and in his habitual references to the cultural and socioeconomic coordinates of his own existence, wherever for the sake of his new science he published illustrations from his own life.

2. Growth and Crises of the Healthy Personality

1. See Part I of the author's *Childhood and Society* (1950a).

2. My participation in the longitudinal research of the Institute of Child Welfare at the University of California (see Macfarlane, 1938; Erikson, 1951b) has taught me the greatest respect for the resiliency and resourcefulness of individual children who, with the support of an expanding economy and of a generous social group, learned to compensate for grievous early misfortunes of a kind which in our clinical histories would suffice to explain malfunctioning rather convincingly. The study gave me an opportunity to chart a decade of the life histories of about fifty (healthy) children, and to remain somewhat informed about the further fortunes of some of them. However, only the development of the identity concept (see this volume, pp. 108–175) has helped me to approach an understanding of the mechanisms involved. I hope to publish my impressions.

3. The reader trained in child development may want to pay special attention to the fact that one can think of a stage as the time when a capacity *first appears* (or appears in testable form) or as that period when it is so well *established* and integrated (has become an available apparatus for the ego, as we would say) that the next step in development can safely be initiated.

4. One of the chief misuses of the schema presented here is the connotation that the sense of trust (and all the other *positive* senses to be postulated) is an *achievement*, secured once and for all at a given stage. In fact, some writers are so intent on making an *achievement scale* out of these stages that they blithely omit all the *negative* senses (basic mistrust, etc.) which are and remain the dynamic counterpart of the positive senses throughout life. (See, for example, the "maturation chart" distributed at the National Congress of Parents and Teachers in Omaha, Nebraska [1958], which omits any reference to crises, and otherwise "adapts" the stages presented here.)

What the child acquires at a given stage is a certain *ratio* between the positive and the negative which, if the balance is toward the positive, will help him to meet later crises with a better chance for unimpaired total development. The idea that at any stage a *goodness* is achieved which is impervious to new conflicts within and changes without is a projection on child development of that success ideology which so dangerously pervades our private and public daydreams and can make us inept in the face of a heightened struggle for a meaningful existence in our time.

Only in the light of man's inner division and social antagonism is a belief in his essential resourcefulness and creativity justifiable and productive.

5. On the wall of a cowboys' bar in the wide-open West hangs a saying: "I ain't what I ought to be, I ain't what I'm going to be, but I ain't what I was."

6. The same is true of "parenthood"—an all too concrete term which, in quotations from this paper, is often used as a replacement for the seemingly more obscure word "generativity." However, in these first formulations the relationship of generativity to work productivity is understated.

3. The Problem of Ego Identity

1. At the 35th Anniversary Institute of the Judge Baker Guidance Center in Boston, May, 1953, and at the Midwinter Meetings of the American Psychoanalytic Association, New York, 1953.

2. ". . . *die klare Bewusstheit der inneren Identität* (Freud, 1926).

3. My italics.

4. Child Guidance Study, Institute of Child Welfare, University of California.

5. William James (1896) speaks of an abandonment of "the old alternative ego," and even of "the murdered self."

6. For a new approach see Anna Freud and Sophie Dann's (1951) report on displaced children.

7. Originally "identity diffusion." It was repeatedly pointed out to me that this term was not a felicitous one. At a meeting of a WHO Study Group, J. Huxley suggested "dispersion" instead. And indeed, the most common meaning of the term "diffusion" is the spatial one of a centrifugal dispersion of elements. In culture diffusion, for example, a technological item, an art form, or an idea may have been transmitted by way of migration, or excursion, or trade contact from one culture to another, often far away. In this use of the term, nothing disorderly or confused is implied; the center does not suffer from such dispersion. In identity diffusion, however, a split of self-images is suggested, a loss of centrality, a sense of dispersion and confusion, and a fear of dissolution. The term "identity confusion," in turn, should continue to denote primarily an acute state of symptomatic upset.

8. See Chapters VIII (Status and Role) and XI (Social Class) in G. H. Mead (1934). For a recent psychoanalytic approach to role and status, see Ackerman (1951).

9. *Wholeness* connotes an assembly of parts, even quite diversified parts, that enter into fruitful association and organization. This concept is most strikingly expressed in such terms as wholeheartedness, wholemindedness, wholesomeness, and the like. As a Gestalt, then, wholeness emphasizes a progressive mutuality between diversified functions and parts. *Totality*, on the contrary, evokes a Gestalt in which an absolute boundary is emphasized: given a certain arbitrary delineation, nothing that belongs inside must be left outside; nothing that must be outside should be tolerated inside. A totality must be as absolutely inclusive as it is absolutely exclusive. The dictionary uses the word "utter" in

this connection. It conveys the element of force, which overrides the question whether the original category-to-be-made-absolute is a logical one, and whether the parts really have, so to speak, a yearning for one another.

There is both in individual and in group psychology a periodical need for a totality without further choice or alternation, even if it implies the abandonment of a much-desired wholeness. To say it in one sentence: Where the human being despairs of an essential wholeness, he restructures himself and the world by taking refuge in totalism.

Psychoanalysis reveals how strong and systematic are man's unconscious *proclivities and potentialities for total realignments*, often barely hidden behind one-sided predilections and convictions, and, on the other hand, how much energy is employed in inner defenses against a threatening total reorientation in which black may turn into white and vice versa. Only the affect released in sudden conversions testifies to the quantity of this energy. (See Erikson, 1953).

10. I owe new insights in this field to Robert Knight (1953) and to Margaret Brenman (1952).

11. David Rapaport's (1953) ego-psychological approach to "activity and passivity" sheds new light on the ego's role in such crises.

12. This example illustrates well the balance which must be found in the interpretation given to such patients between *sexual symbolism* (here castration) which, if overemphasized by the therapist, can only increase the patient's sense of being endangered; and the *representation of dangers to the ego* (here the danger of having the thread of one's autonomy cut off) the communication of which is more urgent, more immediately beneficial, and a condition for the safe discussion of sexual meanings.

13. See, however, Piers and Singer (1953).

14. I am not yet able to establish the systematic convergencies and divergencies between the work of the so-called "Neo-Freudians" and that which I am trying to formulate. It will be seen, however, that in individuals as well as in groups I prefer to speak of a "sense of identity" rather than of a "character structure" or "basic character." In nations, too, my concepts would lead me to concentrate on the conditions and experiences which heighten or endanger a national sense of identity rather than on a static national character. An introduction to this subject is offered in my book *Childhood and Society* (1950a). Here it is important to remember that each identity cultivates its own sense of freedom—wherefore a people rarely understands what makes other peoples feel free. This fact is amply exploited by totalitarian propaganda and underestimated in the Western world.

15. My italics.

16. My italics.

17. See the concern over personal children, patients, and germinating ideas in Freud's "Irma dream" (Erikson, 1954). In my psychosocial interpretation of this dream I pointed out that a dream can be seen to retrace the steps of psychosocial development at the same time that it represents a psychosexual regression to a certain infantile stage of libido development. Freud's dreams (because of the strong inner structure of his personality and maybe also because of the didactic interest with which he went about dreaming them) prove to be continuously enlightening even in regard to matters not explicitly formulated by him, such as the parallelism of psychosocial and psychosexual themes. In the Irma dream, so I showed in my paper, the theme of *phallic* intrusion can be seen to be closely associated with that of *initiative*. Similarly, Freud's dream of the Three Fates clearly points to the close relationship of *oral* incorporation and the problem of *trust*; while the dream of Count Thun strongly emphasizes themes of *autonomy* and the modes of *anal* elimination. A paper comparing these three dreams is in preparation.

18. In this paper, I cannot more than approach the possible relation of the problem of

Notes   185

identity to ideological processes (see Erikson, 1958a), and I can only parenthetically list possible analogous correspondences between stages of psychosocial development in the individual and major trends of social organization. As pointed out in "Growth and Crises of the Healthy Personality" (pp. 67–87), the problem of Autonomy (versus Shame and Doubt) has intrinsic relations with the delineation of individual rights and limitations in the basic principles of law and justice, and the problem of Initiative (versus Guilt) with the encouragements and limitations emanating from the dominant ethos of production. The problem of workmanship critically prepares for the predominant techniques of production and their characteristic division of labor.

19. Organized by Professors S. Eisenstadt and C. Frankenstein of the Hebrew University. The initial impressions presented here are mine.

20. We may state tentatively that the elites which emerge from historical change are groups which out of the deepest common identity crisis manage to create a new style of coping with the outstanding danger situations of their society.

21. I.e., relative communism within the individual community, which, however, in its relation to the national economy, rather represents a capitalist cooperative.

22. We may ask, for example, what inner, unconscious gain the delinquent may derive from a total choice of delinquency as a way or as a goal of life. It is possible that his radical closing up, his provocative smugness, his utter denial of remorse, may cover and counteract the anxiety of threatening identity diffusion. Are we, in turn, exposing him to this very danger as we hammer at him, offering him a "chance" at the price of remorse—the one price that he cannot afford to pay? A glance at the components of identity diffusion (horizontal V, p. 129) will lead to these considerations:

Juvenile delinquency saves some young individuals from *time diffusion*. In the delinquent state, any future perspective, with its demands and uncertainties, is overruled by the dominant emphasis on short-range goals serving, say, a need to "get at somebody," or to just "do something," or "go somewhere." This, of course, also constitutes a simplification of social modalities, together with a primitivization of impulse life.

Identity consciousness is escaped also; or, at any rate, it is firmly hidden by the delinquent's particular identification-with-himself-in-the-role-of-delinquent, which offers such an impenetrable façade to investigator and judge. This façade—the outward appearance of a total choice—denies any emotional response, and prevents the emergence of any sense of shame or guilt.

Work paralysis, the painful inability to enjoy the mastery of materials and of cooperative situations, is also sidetracked in delinquency. Work mastery is in any culture the backbone of identity formation. In delinquents (often recruited from groups who are denied a meaningful work experience) there appears, instead, a perverse but deep satisfaction in "doing a job" in the destructive sense. The legal classification of such a deed may seal a young individual's *negative identity* as a criminal once and for all. This, in turn, relieves him of the necessity to search further for a "good" identity (Erikson and Erikson, 1957).

In addition, delinquent behavior saves many individuals from *bisexual diffusion*. The exaggeration of the phallic-sadistic role on the part of the boy delinquent and the careless and loveless promiscuity on the part of the girl offer an escape either from a sense of sexual inferiority or from any commitment to true intimacy.

In this connection a development highly characteristic of our time must be emphasized: I mean the new emphasis on locomotion, as provided by the machine. There is first of all what might be called the *locomotorist intoxication* of our time—the pleasure of imagining oneself to be an immensely powerful driver, while actually being moved by powers stronger and faster than those of the human body.

The second intoxication (now conveniently combined with the first in drive-in shows) is the passive *intoxication by powerfully moving spectacles*—in which continuous motion is not only observed by experience, while the organism "races its engine," as it were. Since youth is an eminently locomotor period, and since in adolescence perambulatory (as well as mental) exploration must take over much of sexual tension, the disbalance between increased passive stimulation provided by mechanical invention and decreased opportunities for vigorous action is probably a major contributor to such specific delinquencies at the appropriation of motorcars and the urge to do physical violence, and to the widespread addiction to excessive forms of dancing.

As for *authority diffusion*, it is clear that organized delinquency clearly aligns the young person with an ingroup of equals with a defined hierarchy of leadership, and clearly circumscribes outgroups such as other gangs, or all the world outside the gang. Similarly, gang ethics protect the ingroup member from a sense of *diffusion of ideals*.

It is in this way that I would approach the problem of juvenile delinquency with concepts gained from the observation of psychiatric kinds of juvenile disturbance. Such a comparison suggests that we may learn much about the dynamics of youth by juxtaposing the delinquent joiners and the schizoid isolates (even as Freud juxtaposed perversion and neurosis as the expression and the inhibition of certain impulses) (Erikson, 1956).

Bibliography

Ackerman, N. W. (1951), "Social Role" and Total Personality. *Am. J. Ortho-psychiat.*, 21:1–17.

Bateman, J. F., and Dunham, H. W. (1948), The State Mental Hospital as a Specialized Community Experience. *Am. J. Psychiat.*, 105:445–449.

Benedict, R. (1938), Continuities and Discontinuities in Cultural Conditioning. *Psychiatry*, 1:161–167.

Bettelheim, B. (1943), Individual and Mass Behavior in Extreme Situations. *J. Abn. Soc. Psychol.*, 38:417–452.

Bibring, E. (1953), The Mechanism of Depression. In *Affective Disorders*, P. Greenacre, ed. New York: International Universities Press, pp. 13–48.

Blos, P. (1953), The Contribution of Psychoanalysis to the Treatment of Adolescents. In *Psychoanalysis and Social Work*, M. Heiman, ed. New York: International Universities Press.

Brenman, M. (1952), On Teasing and Being Teased: And the Problem of "Moral Masochism." *The Psychoanalytic Study of the Child*, 7:264–285. New York: International Universities Press. Also in *Psychoanalytic Psychiatry and Psychology: Clinical and Theoretical Papers*, Austen Riggs Center, Vol. I, R. P. Knight and C. R. Friedman, eds. New York: International Universities Press, 1954, pp. 29–51.

Burlingham, D. (1952), *Twins.* New York: International Universities Press.

Erikson, E. H. (1937), Configuration in Play—Clinical Notes. *Psa. Quart.*, 6:139–214.

———(1940a), Problems of Infancy and Early Childhood. In *Cyclopedia of Medicine.* Philadelphia: Davis & Co., pp. 714–730. Also in *Outline of Abnormal Psychology*, G. Murphy and A. Bachrach, eds. New York: Modern Library, 1954, pp. 3–36.

—— (1940b), On Submarine Psychology. Written for the Committee on National Morale for the Coordinator of Information. Unpublished ms.

—— (1942), Hitler's Imagery and German Youth. *Psychiatry*, 5:475–493.

——(1945), Childhood and Tradition in Two American Indian Tribes. *The Psychoanalytic Study of the Child*, 1:319–350. New York: International Universities Press. Also (revised) in *Personality in Nature, Society and Culture*, C. Kluckhohn and H. Murray, eds. New York: Knopf, 1948, pp. 176–203.

—— (1946), Ego Development and Historical Change—Clinical Notes. *The Psychoanalytic Study of the Child*, 2:359–396. New York: International Universities Press.

——(1950a), *Childhood and Society*. New York: Norton. Revised, 1963.

—— (1950b), Growth and Crises of the "Healthy Personality." In *Symposium on the Healthy Personality*, Supplement II; Problems of Infancy and Childhood, Transactions of Fourth Conference, March, 1950, M. J. E. Senn, ed. New York: Josiah Macy, Jr. Foundation. Also in *Personality in Nature, Society, and Culture*, 2nd ed., C. Kluckhohn and H. Murray, eds. New York: Knopf, 1953, pp. 185–225.

—— (1951a), On the Sense of Inner Identity. In *Health and Human Relations*; Report on a conference on Health and Human Relations held at Hiddesen near Detmold, Germany, August 2–7, 1951. Sponsored by the Josiah Macy, Jr. Foundation. New York: Blakiston, 1953. Also in *Psychoanalytic Psychiatry and Psychology: Clinical and Theoretical Papers*, Austen Riggs Center, Vol. I, R. P. Knight and C. R. Friedman, eds. New York: International Universities Press, 1954, pp. 351–364.

—— (1951b), Sex Differences in the Play Configurations of Preadolescents. *Am. J. Orthopsychiat.*, 21:667–692.

—— (1953), Wholeness and Totality. In *Totalitarianism*, Proceedings of a conference held at the American Academy of Arts and Sciences, March, 1953, C. J. Friedrich, ed. Cambridge: Harvard University Press, 1954.

—— (1954), The Dream Specimen of Psychoanalysis. *J. Amer. Psa. Assoc.*, 2:5–56, Also in *Psychoanalytic Psychiatry and Psychology: Clinical and Theoretical Papers*, Austen Riggs Center, Vol. I, R. P. Knight and C. R. Friedman, eds. New York: International Universities Press, 1954, pp. 131–170.

—— (1955a), The Syndrome of Identity Diffusion in Adolescents and Young Adults. In *Discussions on Child Development*, J. M. Tanner and B. Inhelder, eds. Vol. III of the Proceedings of the World Health Organization Study Group on the Psychobiological Development of the Child, Geneva, 1955. New York: International Universities Press, 1958, pp. 133–154.

—— (1955b), The Psychosocial Development of Children. In *Discussions on Child Development*, J. M. Tanner and B. Inhelder, eds. Vol. III of the Proceedings of the World Health Organization Study Group on the Psychobiological Development of the Child, Geneva, 1955. New York: International Universities Press, 1958, pp. 169–188.

Bibliography

_____(1956), Ego Identity and the Psychosocial Moratorium. In *New Perspectives for Research in Juvenile Delinquency*, H.L. Witmer and R. Kosinsky, eds. U. S. Children's Bureau: Publication #356, pp. 1–23.

_____(1958a), *Young Man Luther, A Study in Psychoanalysis and History*. New York: Norton.

_____(1958b), The Nature of Clinical Evidence. *Daedalus*, 87:65–87. Also in *Evidence and Interference*, The First Hayden Colloquium. Cambridge: The Technology Press of M.I.T., 1958.

_____(1958c), Identity and Uprootedness in our Time. Address at the Annual Meeting of the World Federation for Mental Health, Vienna.

_____(1964), *Insight and Responsibility*. New York: Norton.

_____(1968), *Identity: Youth and Crisis*. New York: Norton.

_____(1969), *Gandhi's Truth*. New York: Norton.

_____(1974), *Dimensions of a New Identity*. New York: Norton.

_____(1975), *Life History and the Historical Moment*. New York: Norton.

_____(1977), *Toys and Reasons*. New York: Norton.

_____ed. (1978), *Adulthood*. New York: Norton.

_____(in press), Elements of a Psychoanalytic Theory of Psychosocial Development. In *The Course of Life*, S. I. Greenspan and G. H. Pollock, eds. Adelphi, Md.: National Institute of Mental Health.

_____and Erikson, K. (1957), The Confirmation of the Delinquent. *Chicago Review*, Winter, pp. 15–23.

Erikson, K. T. (1957), Patient-Role and Social Uncertainty—a Dilemma of the Mentally Ill. *Psychiatry*, 20:263–274.

Federn, P. (1927–1949), *Ego Psychology and the Psychoses*. New York: Basic Books, 1952.

Fenichel, O. (1945), *The Psychoanalytic Theory of Neurosis* New York: Norton.

Freud, A. (1936), *The Ego and the Mechanisms of Defence*. New York: International Universities Press, 1946.

_____(1945), Indications for Child Analysis. *The Psychoanalytic Study of the Child*, 1:127–149. New York: International Universities Press.

_____and Dann, S. (1951), An Experiment in Group Upbringing. *The Psychoanalytic Study of the Child*, 6:127–168. New York: International Universities Press.

Freud, S. (1908), "Civilized" Sexual Morality and Modern Nervousness. *Collected Papers*, 2:76–99. London: Hogarth, 1948.

_____(1914), On Narcissism: An Introduction. *Standard Edition*, 14:73–102 London: Hogarth, 1957. New York: Norton.

_____(1926), Ansprache an die Mitglieder des Vereins B'nai B'rith. *Gesammelte Werke*, 17:49–53. London: Imago, 1941.

_____(1932), *New Introductory Lecutres on Psychoanalysis*. Lecture 31: The Anatomy of the Mental Personality. New York: Norton, 1933.

_____(1938), *An Outline of Psychoanalysis*. New York: Norton, 1949.

Bibliography

Fromm-Reichmann, F. (1950), *Principles of Intensive Psychotherapy*. Chicago: University of Chicago Press.

Ginsburg, S. W. (1954), The Role of Work. *Samiksa*, 8:1–13.

Hartmann, H. (1939), *Ego Psychology and the Problem of Adaptation*. New York: International Universities Press, 1958. Also in *Organization and Pathology of Thought*, D. Rapaport, ed. New York: Columbia University Press: 1951.

——— (1950), Comments on the Psychoanalytic Theory of the Ego. *The Psychoanalytic Study of the Child*, 5:74–96. New York: International Universities Press.

——— and Kris, E. (1945), The Genetic Approach in Psychoanalysis. *The Psychoanalytic Study of the Child*, 1:11–30. New York: International Universities Press.

———, ———, and Loewenstein, R. M. (1951), Some Psychoanalytic Comments on "Culture and Personality." In *Psychoanalysis and Culture*, G. B. Wilbur and W. Muensterberger, eds. New York: International Universities Press, pp. 3–31.

Hendrick, I. (1943), Work and the Pleasure Principle. *Psa. Quart.*, 12:311–329.

Jahoda, M. (1950), Toward a Social Psychology of Mental Health. In *Symposium on the Healthy Personality*, Supplement II; Problems of Infancy and Childhood, Transactions of Fourth Conference, March, 1950, M. J. E. Senn, ed. New York: Josiah Macy, Jr. Foundation.

James, W. (1896), The Will to Believe. *New World*, 5:327–347.

Kinsey, A. C., Pomeroy, W. B., and Martin, C. E. (1948), *Sexual Behavior in the Human Male*. Philadelphia: Saunders.

Knight, R. P. (1953), Management and Psychotherapy of the Borderline Schizophrenic Patient. *Bull. Menninger Clin.*, 17:139–150. Also in *Psychoanalytic Psychiatry and Psychology: Clinical and Theoretical Papers*, Austen Riggs Center, Vol. I, R. P. Knight and C. R. Friedman, eds. New York: International Universities Press, 1954, pp. 110–122.

Kris, E. (1952), *Psychoanalytic Explorations in Art*. New York: International Universities Press.

Macfarlane, J. W. (1938), Studies in Child Guidance. I. Methodology of Data Collection and Organization. *Monogs. Society for Research in Child Development*, Vol. 3, No. 6.

Mannheim, K. (1949), *Utopia and Ideology*. New York: Harcourt, Brace.

Mead, G. H. (1934), *Mind, Self, and Society*. Chicago: University of Chicago Press.

Mead, M. (1949), *Male and Female*. New York: Morrow.

National Congress of Parents and Teachers (1958), *Breaking Through the Limiting Circle of Immaturity*. The Headquarters of the National Congress of Parents and Teachers, 700 North Rush Street, Chicago.

Nunberg, H. (1931), The Synthetic Function of the Ego, *Int. J. Psa.*, 12:123–140. Also in *Practice and Theory of Psychoanalysis*. New York: International Universities Press, 1955, pp. 120–136.

Piers, G., and Singer, M. B. (1953), *Shame and Guilt*. New York: Norton.

Rapaport, D. (1953), Some Metapsychological Considerations Concerning Activity and Passivity. Two lectures given at the staff seminar of the Austen Riggs Center. Unpublished ms.

———(1957–1958), A Historical Survey of Psychoanalytic Ego Psychology. *Bulletin of the Philadelphia Association for Psychoanalysis.* 7/8: 105–120.

Riesman, D. (1950), *The Lonely Crowd*. New Haven: Yale University Press.

Schilder, P. (1930–1940), *Psychoanalysis, Man, and Society*. New York: Norton, 1951.

———(1934), *The Image and Appearance of the Human Body*. New York: International Universities Press, 1951.

Schwartz, M. S., and Will, G. T. (1953), Low Morale and Mutual Withdrawal on a Mental Hospital Ward. *Psychiatry*, 16:337–353.

Shaw, G. B. (1952), *Selected Prose*. New York: Dodd, Mead.

Spitz, R. A. (1945), Hospitalism. *The Psychoanalytic Study of the Child*, 1:53–74. New York: International Universities Press.

Spock, B. (1945), *The Common Sense Book of Baby and Child Care*. New York: Duell, Sloan & Pearce.

Sullivan, H. S. (1946–1947), *The Interpersonal Theory of Psychiatry*. New York: Norton, 1953.

Zilboorg, G. (1944), Present Trends in Psychoanalytic Theory and Practice. *Bull. Menninger Clin.*, 8:3–8.